# GAME OF MY LIFE

## PITTSBURGH

## STEELERS

# GAME OF MY LIFE

## PITTSBURGH

## STEELERS

MEMORABLE STORIES OF STEELERS FOOTBALL

MATT LOEDE

SPORTS
PUBLISHING

Sports Publishing books may be purchased in bulk at special discounts for sales promotion, corporate gifts, fund-raising, or educational purposes. Special editions can also be created to specifications. For details, contact the Special Sales Department, Sports Publishing, 307 West 36th Street, 11th Floor, New York, NY 10018 or sportspubbooks@skyhorsepublishing.com.

Sports Publishing® is a registered trademark of Skyhorse Publishing, Inc.®, a Delaware corporation.

Visit our website at www.sportspubbooks.com.

10 9 8 7 6 5 4 3 2 1

Library of Congress Cataloging-in-Publication Data is available on file.

Cover design by Tom Lau
Cover photo credit Associated Press

ISBN: 978-1-61321-814-3
Ebook ISBN: 978-1-61321-854-9

Printed in the United States of America

# CONTENTS

# INTRODUCTION

The Pittsburgh Steelers are one of the greatest franchises in not only the NFL, but in all of sports. Since the dawn of the Super Bowl era, the team has won an NFL record six championships, and has appeared in two other Super Bowls in losing efforts. The early years of the franchise were not so pretty, as the club from 1933 to 1971 played in just two playoff games, losing both, the first in 1947 and the second in 1962. It wasn't until Art Rooney hired Chuck Noll, a Baltimore Colts assistant coach, that the franchise finally started to reach the heights that fans had been waiting for.

Noll's arrival along with the drafting of some of the greatest players in NFL history turned the team around, and by 1974 the club reached its first Super Bowl, beating the Minnesota Vikings 16-6 in New Orleans. They won their next Super Bowl the next season topping the Dallas Cowboys 21-17 in Miami.

After a two-year hiatus, the Steelers won Super Bowls XIII and XIV, beating Dallas and the Los Angeles Rams to complete their 1970s dynasty with four Super Bowl titles, a record that stood until dynasties by the Dallas Cowboys and San Francisco 49ers.

Following the final championship in 1979, the team went into a bit of a downturn in the 1980s, as the Hall of Fame players from the '70s like Joe Greene, Jack Lambert, Terry Bradshaw, Mel Blount, Jack Ham, and others stepped away from the game.

The team's drafting in the 1980s was nowhere near as good as in the 1970s, and the records suffered. The Steelers did reach the AFC Title Game in 1984 and the postseason in 1989, but those were the final two seasons a Chuck Noll–coached team would play beyond the regular season.

Noll retired after the 1991 season, giving way to a fiery young leader in Bill Cowher, who came to the Steelers from the Kansas City Chiefs. Cowher was a linebacker with the Cleveland Browns and Philadelphia Eagles, and the "players' coach" style he took to the team and fiery attitude energized fans both young and old.

Cowher took the team to Super Bowl XXX in 1995, a losing effort to the Dallas Cowboys. It seemed like he was snake bitten as he took the club to six AFC Title Games, but fell short in four of those six games, with all four losses coming at home. But he finally got the Steelers back to the Super Bowl after the 2005 season in a memorable ride with Jerome "The Bus" Bettis—a win over the Seattle Seahawks 21-10 in Detroit in Super Bowl XL.

A year after winning Super Bowl XL, Cowher retired after fifteen seasons, and the team hired Mike Tomlin, an intense young leader who took the team to a win in Super Bowl XLIII in just his second season in Pittsburgh, clinching the team's NFL record sixth title.

Since that team walked off the field in Tampa in 2009 with their sixth title, they have been trying to get back to winning a seventh championship. The club did get to the Super Bowl in the 2010 season, but lost to the Green Bay Packers in a wild game in Dallas.

Tomlin appreciates the history of the franchise, and knows the high standard that the Steelers to this day stand by. Every year, he and the coaches expect to win, and the fan base has been spoiled by the years of some of the greatest players in NFL history.

The twenty-three players I interviewed for this book offer an array of great stories and great memories. From exhibition games that started players' careers to memorable regular season games to playoff battles and Super Bowls, the players I spoke to shared some of the best memories of Steelers football from the past four decades.

I hope you enjoy reading this book as much as I enjoyed talking to the players and writing it.

# CHAPTER 1

# MERRIL HOGE

### Running Back 1987–1993

### December 31, 1989 vs Houston Oilers at Houston Astrodome

### PITTSBURGH STEELERS 26 - HOUSTON OILERS 23

Most of the younger Pittsburgh Steelers fans know Merril Hoge for his work each week as a football analyst for ESPN, being vocal in sharing his thoughts about the ins and outs of the NFL on a weekly basis.

What they don't know is that there was a time, back in early 1990, when for two games Hoge's NFL career went from mostly obscurity to a Cinderella story for the playoff run of the 1989 Steelers.

The 1989 season was possibly the best coaching job in the Hall-of-Fame career of Steelers coach Chuck Noll, as he took the team from the first two games in which they were outscored 92-10 to a point away from playing in the AFC Championship Game.

The season started with a 51-0 home loss in the opener to the Cleveland Browns, and then a 41-10 road loss to the Cincinnati Bengals.

The day after the Bengals loss there was a number of national stories that wondered if Noll was going to last the season, and if the team was actually the worst in the NFL.

The team did turn it around, and Hoge recalls that season with great fondness for all the things he learned at the time as a twenty-four-year-old running back in just his third NFL season.

"That year was most memorable for a lot of reasons," Hoge said. "I learned a lot about leadership, about how when things are going south how you recover and what things you can lean on."

*AP Photo*

## Notes on Merril Hoge

| | |
|---|---|
| **Years Played:** | 1987–1993 |
| **Position:** | Running Back |
| **Height:** | 6'2" |
| **Weight:** | 212 |
| **Hometown:** | Pocatello, Idaho |
| **Current Residence:** | Fort Thomas, Kentucky |
| **Occupation:** | Broadcaster for ESPN |
| **Accomplishments:** | Played eight seasons in the NFL, seven with the Steelers, one with the Chicago Bears. Was the Steelers 10th-round pick of the 1987 NFL Draft. In NFL career put up 3,139 yards rushing, 2,133 receiving and 34 touchdowns. Best known for his play during the 1989 playoff run by the Steelers, in which an AFC Wild Card Game win over the Houston Oilers he ran for 100 yards on 17 carries and a touchdown in a 26-23 overtime win. The following week in a loss to the Denver Broncos in the AFC Divisional Playoff Game, Hoge ran for 120 yards and a score, and caught eight passes for 60 yards. He has served on the board of directors of the Highmark Caring Foundation since the early '90s. |
| **Nickname:** | None |
| **The Game:** | Pittsburgh Steelers vs Houston Oilers in Houston, Texas<br>December 31, 1989 |

"We got beat 92-10 in the first two games and we were the laughing stock of the NFL," Hoge said. "There was a ton of articles out on us, about what a bad team we were. I remember Chuck the first Tuesday after that second game, and he was reading to us all the things people were saying about us.

"He said 'Listen, I know nobody believes in you, I know no one thinks you're any good, but I want you to know, I do. I believe in you.'

"I could feel the energy in the room completely change. His leadership in that process was instrumental. I only got to play for him for five years, but I look back at that year and use a lot of those life lessons to this day."

Hoge was a 10th round draft pick of the Steelers in 1987 out of Idaho State, where he was a three-time all-conference selection at running back.

\* \* \*

He played mostly special teams in 1987, but by 1988 he had earned an opportunity with the franchise to be a main part of their offense, starting eight games and running for 705 yards and three touchdowns. The 1988 season saw the club go just 5-11, but it will be most remembered for the club losing their beloved owner, Art Rooney, just a month before the start of the season.

The 1989 season saw Hoge have another productive regular season, rushing for 621 yards and eight scores.

The team at 9-7 found its way to the playoffs after a number of things went their way in the last week of the season that clinched them a wild card playoff spot.

The wild card opponent was one the team and Hoge knew well, the rival Houston Oilers. A team that had beaten the Steelers twice during the regular season in 1989.

There was a long-running feud between Steelers coach Chuck Noll and Oilers coach Jerry Glanville.

While a lot of the focus was on the two coaches in the 1989 AFC Wild Card Game in Houston, it was Hoge's star that would shine the brightest on one of the biggest stages in the NFL.

# The Game
*By Merril Hoge*

The game that really stands out in most people's minds was in '89 with the Oilers, and then the following we week we went to Denver, those back-to-back weeks, those were probably the two most significant games I've ever played in.

That Houston game wild card weekend would fall in the top 5 or 10 in NFL history.

There's so many things about that game that happened that people probably have forgotten. The game itself was obviously itself a special game.

I don't think people would know or remember that game ended [Oilers coach] Jerry Glanville's career.

That was instrumental because the start of my career, my rookie year was the first time I had ever played in Houston, and that was the start of the feud between Glanville and Chuck Noll.

That feud started in 1987, I know our offense was on the field and it involved our running back, Frank Pollard.

He got into a fight with someone on their defensive line, and Glanville sent players out from the sideline and they basically blindsided Frank Pollard and took him out.

What the discrepancy was is—it wasn't the guys getting into a fight on the field, it was Glanville sending players from the sideline to go after one of our players.

I was standing right there when it happened. Chuck Noll had come across the field, and went right to Jerry Glanville when it happened.

He reached out and grabbed Jerry Glanville's hand and let him know, "If you ever send anyone from the sideline again onto the field after one of my players, I'm coming after you." Jerry Glanville didn't really know how to respond to it. He was just in shock and just starts to walk away. Chuck grabs him and pulls him back and says, "I'm serious, you son of a b#@ch." I was already ready to run through a brick wall for that man, now I'll do whatever I have to do for him. I got his back, because that guy has our back.

We went to the locker room and Chuck talked about that moment. He said "Listen, we don't start fights, that's not how we play. That's not

5

how we perform; that's not how you be a professional. But, don't you ever let one of our guys be assaulted. You defend yourself and you defend one another."

Glanville made a snide remark every time we went to play them. He kept revisiting that, while Chuck never talked about it, never revisited it.

They beat us twice that year, they beat us at home and we thought that loss to them was going to knock us out of the playoffs.

We went down and won in Tampa in the final week and got a bunch of miracles to get back in the playoffs.

Chuck had won coach of the year in 1989, and during that week, the wild card week, Glanville says, "I voted for Chuck for coach of the year, I spelled his name Knoll." He said it just to be a jerk, just to be a jerk.

They had the "House of Pain" going on; they had bounties out on people. They were trying to knock people out on kickoffs.

They always had one of the most talented teams in the NFL, and they always seemed to have a winning record in the regular season.

There was a bunch of things that went on in that game. I remember Chuck Noll, who was so adamant about their offense, the "run and shoot," and he told us, "Look guys the run and shoot is good from 20 to 20, but once they get inside the 20 it's a different game." I remember listening to him talk about that offense, and how it almost exactly happened in that game.

There was a few things that happened at the end of that game that were most fascinating. It was probably the most exhausted I've ever been in any game at any time.

It was my first playoff experience, and you could really sense the difference. It was just completely different.

I don't care if it was first, second, or third down, the weight of that down was so important.

We got the lead, and they rallied back and took the lead. We had a drive to tie the game, and that drive, I remember there was a TV timeout, and we literally could not hear.

Bubby [Brister] was getting all fired up, he was just giving us a tongue lashing while we were in the huddle.

You almost had to read his lips to hear the play. Early in that drive we called a reverse to Dwight Stone, he was so fast, and that really kick-started that drive.

I went over the top to score to tie the game at 23. I had a play earlier in the drive to help us, and Bubby hit four out of five passes in the drive.

When we went into overtime, we got the ball and we went three-and-out. Harry Newsome, our punter, had a real bad punt, and they had the ball near midfield.

They gave the ball to Lorenzo White, and Rod Woodson came up and hit him right on the ball. White fumbled and Rod picked it up and was tackled pretty quickly but we got the ball back around the 50.

The very first play they called was "93-trap" and I went about 14 yards to put us in field goal range. That was the last yard we got.

I was sweating so much that I was "slushing" in my shoes; my socks and shoes were so soaking wet it was like I jumped in a pond.

I went to the sideline and took a knee, and my pads just fell off of me. I was drenched.

This is how delirious I was: I remember thinking, "I have nothing left."

Gary [Anderson] was lining up for a 50-yard field goal, and I remember looking up at the screen on the scoreboard and reading, "This is Gary Anderson's first attempt at a 50-yard field goal." I'm soaking wet, physically I can't even move, I'm thinking if he doesn't make this I have no shot of running another play. I'm on one knee, I don't even know how I'm getting to the locker room.

Then I start thinking, "Gary Anderson is as old as dirt, he's never kicked a 50-yard field goal?" I'm thinking, "Are you freaking kidding me, there's no way he's going to make it!" Then I happen to look up at the screen, and there's a few words I didn't read— "First attempt at a 50-yard field goal—this year." That completely changed me then, I'm like, "Oh yeah he's got a shot." So they snap the ball and he kicks it and it goes through the uprights. All that energy I didn't think I had—I found a little bit of it.

The joy that came through me was crazy.

We look back on the video, the funniest thing when I think about it. Delton Hall, who was our rookie of the year had broken his wrist. He wasn't the player he was our rookie year, and he was kind of in and out of the lineup that year.

He had a personal foul in that game that gave them life when we had him stopped. He had hit Ernest Givins after a pass. Delton was known for doing a knucklehead move here and there.

The footage after we win, Delton Hall is trying to pick up Chuck Noll like we just won the Super Bowl.

You see Chuck slapping away at Delton when he's trying to pick him up, and the next day we're watching the tape and saying, "What were you thinking?" First, it's a wild card game, and second there's no one to help you, and third, you're grabbing Chuck Noll—it was just the funniest thing you'd ever see.

You look over at Jerry Glanville's face when that ball went through the uprights, and you knew it was over.

I don't ever like to see anyone get fired, but the satisfaction that came from that proves that class will always trump being a punk.

Chuck Noll is on the Mount Rushmore of NFL coaching, and you're going to take shots at him? Why not learn?

The Jerry Glanville era was over. (Glanville was fired one week later, on January 6, 1990.)

The way that stadium was built, to get to the locker room they had to close off certain ramps for the fans that were leaving.

So any delay getting from the field, an interview or something, you would have to fight through the crowd to get to the locker room.

I get held up with all these interviews on the field, and I'm the only guy left out there. As I get set to go up the ramps to the locker room, somebody has a huge mug of beer and throws it in my face.

My eyes are stinging, I'm gagging on it. I get to the locker room and they are praying. So I kneel down and Dick Hoak, my running back coach, I grab his hand and he says, "You already drinking?"

I told him, "No, coach. I just got smashed with a bunch of beer from the fans." I was soaking wet from beer, I smelled like a frigging brewery.

That game had a ton of little stories like that.

## The Aftermath

The week after Hoge and the Steelers defeated the Oilers, the team traveled to Denver to play the AFC's number one seed, the Denver Broncos.

Hoge again played like a man on a mission, as he had his best game of the season, going for 120 yards against the Broncos defense, scoring a touchdown as the team built a 17-7 lead.

As the Broncos normally did back in those days, they rallied back, and took a 24-23 lead in the game, with future Hall of Fame quarterback John Elway picking his way through the Steelers defense in the second half to take the lead.

With one last shot, a fumble on a shotgun snap from center proved to finish the Steelers' last chance, and end a playoff run that many Steelers fans still look back on to this day.

Hoge stayed with the Steelers through the 1993 season, opening holes for single season all-time leading rusher Barry Foster in 1992 as Foster went for 1,690 yards in Bill Cowher's first season as the team's head coach.

The offseason following the 1993 campaign, Hoge signed a free agent deal with the Chicago Bears. After suffering multiple concussions, he left the game after just five games played in the 1994 season.

In his career, Hoge gained 3,139 rushing yards and 2,133 receiving yards. He scored 34 touchdowns.

He made the move from the field to the broadcast booth, joining on with the Steelers Radio Network and being the third man in the booth along with Bill Hillgrove and Myron Cope.

"I was the first player to ever be in the booth for the Steelers," Hoge said. "Myron Cope was in there at the time, and Myron was not a fan of any player being in there, and as good as a relationship as we had when we played, he made it difficult on me.

"If you ever listen to any of the games I did with them in 1995 and '96, you never hear me. I would go a whole quarter and not say boo.

"I was there to learn. I have great respect for Myron, I just wanted to learn and add where I could. It just wasn't something he was a fan of."

Hoge used that time in the Steelers booth to learn his craft and then move to ESPN, where he moved to TV and can still be seen to this day giving his opinion on the NFL.

The former Steelers running back was diagnosed with stage II Non-Hodgkin lymphoma in 2003, and after a long battle was able to overcome it, showing once again his fighting spirit that made him one of the most popular backs in the history of the Steelers franchise.

# CHAPTER 2

# CRAIG WOLFLEY

**Offensive Lineman 1980–1989**

**December 30, 1984 vs Denver Broncos at Mile High Stadium**

**PITTSBURGH STEELERS 24 - DENVER BRONCOS 17**

Craig Wolfley still roams the Pittsburgh Steelers sidelines during the season, but now does it with a microphone in his hand as part of the teams radio network as the club's official sideline reporter.

The former offensive lineman came to the Steelers in 1980 as a fifth-round draft pick, and played twelve seasons in the NFL, ten with the Steelers and his final two with the Minnesota Vikings.

Wolfley played college football at Syracuse, and in 1999 was honored by being named to the Syracuse University Football All-Century Team.

Not only was Wolfley a star on the gridiron, he also starred in the world of weight lifting, boxing, martial arts, and sumo wrestling.

In 1981, Wolfely placed fifth in the World's Strongest Man competition, and in 1985 he placed second in the first ever North American professional sumo wrestling tournament. Years later in 2002, he jumped into the ring with famous boxer "Butterbean" Eric Esch, who was known for his thundering knockouts, and was defeated in a four-round match.

Football runs deep in the Wolfley family, as his brother Ron is a former running back with the Arizona Cardinals. Both brothers jumped into broadcasting after retiring. Ron is the color man for the Arizona

## Notes on Craig Wolfley

| | |
|---|---|
| **Years Played:** | 1980–1989 |
| **Position:** | Offensive Lineman |
| **Height:** | 6'1" |
| **Weight:** | 265 |
| **Hometown:** | Buffalo, New York |
| **Current Residence:** | Pittsburgh, Pennsylvania |
| **Occupation:** | Sideline Reporter and Broadcaster for the Pittsburgh Steelers Radio Network |
| **Accomplishments:** | Was drafted by the Steelers in the fifth round, 138th pick overall, of the 1980 draft. Played for Hall of Fame Chuck Noll all of his ten seasons in Pittsburgh, and played his final two seasons with the Minnesota Vikings. Was part of the last three Noll teams clubs to make the postseason: 1982, 1984, and 1989. Also competed in both the World's Strongest Man and the NFL's Strongest Man competitions, boxed professionally and placed second in the first professional Sumo contest held on the North American continent. He holds a black belt in Freestyle Jiu Jitsu and has over nineteen years of martial arts training. Was picked as a member of the Steelers All-Century Team in 2000, as voted online by Pittsburgh fans as a "team" of the best players to ever wear a Steeler uniform. |
| **Nickname:** | None |
| **The Game:** | Pittsburgh Steelers vs Denver Broncos in Denver, Colorado<br>December 30, 1984 |

Cardinals Radio Network. The two had the honor of being on opposing sidelines for Super Bowl XLIII, as the Steelers defeated the Cardinals 27-23.

Wolfley was a team player who never made headlines, but always gave his best on the field and was well liked by his fellow linemen such as Hall of Fame center Mike Webster and Tunch Ilkin. Wolfley shares a close bond with Ilkin to this day.

*Courtesy of the Pittsburgh Steelers*

## The Game

*By Craig Wolfley*

December 30, 1984, in Denver, a divisional playoff game, we were 9-7 that year, and we had beaten the Raiders to get in the playoffs in a must-win, a real bloodbath out in Oakland two weeks before that.

It was great, it was the week before Christmas and Myron Cope, the Steelers broadcaster, was singing, "Deck the Broncos, they're just Yonkos." It was a great, great Christmas song, just hilarious.

That was my first time playing in Mile High [Stadium], and I remember the big speech that Chuck [Noll] gave us on Friday on how if you are in town less than twenty-four hours then the altitude wouldn't affect you. He gave us a big speech on that.

The night before the game, we went out to eat, Tunch, myself, and a couple other offensive linemen, and the whole conversation by fans was "bring on the fish," because they all thought Denver would beat us and move on to play Miami in the AFC Championship. They knew we were there and they were talking, just muted but loud enough so we could hear, and they were saying, "Why are we even bothering playing these guys?" We started off the day going out for pregame warmups, and after about three minutes I staggered up to my conditioning coach Walt Evans and I grabbed him by the throat and I said, "Chuck lied."

It was so funny, it was just unbelievable. I told him try to get some duct tape because I was going to tape the oxygen tank to my back.

We went back in and coach Noll gave us, what was for him, a very impassioned, about seven-minute pregame talk that basically amounted to whoever commits the least amount of turnovers was going to win the game.

So then we went out and fumbled away our first two drives. Mike Webster, Tunch Ilkin, and myself were going off the field and [Webster] "Webby" turns to us and goes, "Okay men what's plan B?" It was just unbelievable, the defense came out and they just played great, they sacked [Broncos QB John] Elway four times.

At one point Elway threw this middle screen and our nose tackle, Gary Dunn, who we lovingly nicknamed "Fat Albert," intercepted the ball and he took about a step and a half and was tackled immediately.

So the comment after the game—his locker wasn't far from mine—to a reporter was, "Yeah if I had cut outside I would have taken it all the way." He didn't even get two steps with the ball; it was so funny.

The biggest thing I remember was in the fourth quarter, I noticed it for the first time, the people doing the "Mile High stomp."

Mile High Stadium was the loudest outdoor venue I ever played in. I am sure Seattle with everything they have going on now is louder, but the fans at Mile High would do this "boom, boom, clap" and stomp their feet, and I remember in the fourth quarter on that final drive in the huddle, we were bunched so tight we couldn't hear, even though [Steelers QB Mark] Malone was screaming at us in the huddle.

I remember during a timeout feeling the vibrations of the "Mile High stomp" under my feet, it was like a madhouse.

We were able to drive down that final drive and win it; it was just powerful.

We had this great resolve, and I remember listening to the national media, and for a lot of guys there was a lot of talk about, "Man can you believe nobody thinks we have a chance here?"

It was just something that stuck in our craw, and really it was a point where I just think you put your feet down and say, "We're not chump change."

## The Aftermath

The game against the Broncos in the 1984 AFC Divisional Playoffs still rates very high among many Steelers fans as one of the best all-time playoff wins. While it didn't lead to an eventual Super Bowl title, the win showed the heart and determination of a team that was not expected to put up much of a fight and knock off a much more heavily favored team in a tough environment.

The following week the Steelers "Cinderella" season ended with a 45-28 setback to the AFC Champion Miami Dolphins, who were led at the time by a young, future Hall of Fame QB named Dan Marino.

The threesome of Marino and wideouts Mark Clayton and Mark Duper torched the Steelers secondary for nine catches for 243 yards and three touchdowns.

Marino finished the day going 21-for-32 for 421 yards with four touchdown throws and one interception.

While again heavy underdogs in that AFC Title loss, the Steelers actually took a 14-10 second quarter lead on a Mark Malone-to-John Stallworth 65-yard touchdown pass. With a quick-strike from Marino to Duper, the Dolphins took the lead back for good on a 41-yard score before the half to make it 17-14.

"We were going on long drives, and I remember even on 3rd and long we were running the ball and getting first downs," Wolfley said.

"They couldn't stop us and we're just grinding in this Miami heat, and I remember then Marino would come back and three passes and it was a touchdown.

"Mike Webster was standing on the sidelines and I remember he threw some Gatorade on the field and he screamed at the defense, 'Slow 'em down a little! I'm trying to get a drink!'"

In order to get the right to play the Broncos in that AFC Divisional Game, the Steelers had to win a tough game the final week of the regular season in Los Angeles against the defending champion Raiders.

In a slugfest reminiscent of the Steelers-Raiders games of the 1970s, the Steelers defense stuffed Los Angeles, holding the Raiders to just 185 yards. Pittsburgh topped the Raiders 13-7 to win the AFC Central with a 9-7 record.

"I remember the brutality of that game," Wolfely recalls. "It was one of those games all of us would have to take out a second mortgage to pay for the fines in today's game."

Wolfley stayed with the Steelers till following the 1989 season, and went on to play two more years in Minnesota with the Vikings.

The offensive lineman was selected as a member of the "Pittsburgh Steelers All-Century Team," which was voted on by Steelers fans as a team of the best players to ever wear a Steelers uniform.

Not only does Wolfley serve as the Steelers sideline reporter for all their games, but he also co-hosts a show with longtime friend and former teammate Tunch Ilkin on ESPN 970 in Pittsburgh.

# CHAPTER 3

# CHARLIE BATCH

### Quarterback 2002–2012

**September 7, 2006 vs Miami Dolphins at Heinz Field**

**PITTSBURGH STEELERS 28 - MIAMI DOLPHINS 17**

Charlie Batch had an opportunity that most could only dream of: playing for the hometown team he grew up watching.

The native of Homestead, PA, got that chance when he joined the Pittsburgh Steelers as their backup quarterback in 2002, and for eleven seasons he was as reliable as any backup quarterback in the NFL, always being ready when called upon.

Batch started his pro career in Detroit with the Lions in 1998, coming off a record-setting college career at Eastern Michigan.

The QB had the luxury of having a Hall of Fame running back in Detroit in Barry Sanders, but the surprise retirement of Sanders in 1999 put Batch as the focus of the Lions offense. Predictably, after losing such a great player, the team struggled.

Batch started 37 games for the Lions his first three seasons, going 19-18. It was the 2001 season that saw Batch assume a true starting role in the NFL for the first time. That year he started nine games, going 0-9 for Detroit as the team limped to a 2-14 season.

That offseason Batch was released by Detroit, and inked a one-year deal with the Steelers. Batch had no guarantee that he would be around

AP Photo/Tony Dejak

## Notes on Charlie Batch

**Years Played:** 2002–2012

**Position:** Quarterback

**Height:** 6'2"

**Weight:** 220

**Hometown:** Homestead, Pennsylvania

**Current Residence:** Pittsburgh, Pennsylvania

**Occupation:** Broadcaster for KDKA-TV in Pittsburgh and Color Analyst for WPIAL high school football and basketball broadcasts

**Accomplishments:** Second-round pick of the Detroit Lions in 1998, and started games for the Lions between '98 and 2001. Signed with the Steelers in 2002 and stayed as the backup quarterback for 11 seasons. Was the backup on two Super Bowl teams, winning rings for Super Bowl XL and XLIII. At the time of him leaving the team, his tenure was the second-longest in team history for a quarterback, behind only Hall of Famer Terry Bradshaw. Won a critical game in Week 12 of the 2012 season, beating the Baltimore Ravens on the road 23–20 in what turned out to be the last start of his NFL career. In his career threw for 11,085 yards, 61 touchdowns, and 52 interceptions. Was the "Whizzer" White NFL Man of the Year in 2012.

**Nickname:** None

**The Game:** Pittsburgh Steelers vs Miami Dolphins, Pittsburgh, Pennsylvania
September 7, 2006

for long as he was on the depth chart behind quarterbacks Kordell Stewart and Tommy Maddox.

Batch stayed around, though, for that season and for ten more with the Steelers. Although in the background, he was always ready to go when needed at the quarterback spot. Batch also provided much needed knowledge as the backup quarterback, giving needed advice to any Steelers quarterback under center.

The QB started nine games for the Steelers in those eleven years, winning six of the nine starts. In his last year with the Steelers in 2012, he won a memorable game on the road in Baltimore that was a huge highlight to the team's season.

Batch's finest moment came in 2006, as the QB made a start on the biggest stage of them all, the opening game of the season on Thursday night against the Miami Dolphins.

## The Game
*By Charlie Batch*

I think the one game that stands out to me was coming out of the [2005] Super Bowl victory to start the 2006 season, the Miami game.

I didn't know I was going to even start the game until basically two days beforehand. You know Ben [Roethlisberger] had gotten into the [motorcycle] accident early in the summer, and he was playing in the preseason so I had anticipated him starting in that particular game.

Then two days before the game he goes in for an emergency appendectomy, and it went from everybody preparing for Ben to then all the sudden it was, "Oh, by the way—Charlie is starting."

Bill Cowher came up and said, "We are riding with you, nothing is changing, we are going to go out and win this ball game." I prepared as if I was the starter all week, the only difference was I didn't get the physical reps. I knew the game plan, I wasn't concerned about the game plan, it's just if you know you are starting on Sunday you at least get the practice reps during the week.

Unfortunately, I wasn't able to get the practice reps during the week because Ben was okay all the way through until two days before the game.

The team had confidence in me, now it was up to me just to go out and play. It was a bigger stage than one you would have for just a normal regular season game because it was the opening Thursday night game.

[We were] coming off the Super Bowl victory, Jerome [Bettis] coming back after retiring and coming back into the stadium, and here we are Super Bowl champions and all eyes were on us this first Thursday night.

People were unsure what we were going to do. Miami had gone out and gotten Daunte Culpepper in the offseason to play quarterback, so it was almost like now everything had shifted to Miami because no one had expected much of us without Ben.

At that particular time I was able to go in and step in during that game and I threw Nate Washington his first touchdown pass, I remember that one. That was the first touchdown of the 2006 regular season.

Then I recall throwing Santonio Holmes his first NFL reception to start his NFL career. I remember those two young receivers in that particular moment.

As the game went on, the thing that stands out to me in that game was throwing, in the fourth quarter, with about seven minutes to go in that game, an 87-yard touchdown pass to Heath Miller.

The funny part about that play was we were sitting on the sideline and [offensive coordinator] Ken Whisenhunt gave me a play, and he kind of looked and it was a play-action pass and I said, "I really don't think they are going to bite on play-action when we are sitting on our 13-yard line, I just don't see that." So Ken said, "Okay, give me another play, what do you think about this?" I told him, "I don't really like that play." He said, "Well damn, what play do you like?!"

I said, "Actually Whis, in this situation I like 126 pass star saint." And he looked at me and said, "126 pass star saint?" I said, "Yeah, it gives me multiple options for that particular play if the first read isn't there." He said, "All right, fine, we'll go out with 126 pass star saint." We went out and sure enough they busted coverage and left Heath Miller wide open on a corner route.

Heath caught the ball and had about 50 yards to go and I was thinking he's got a chance to score. As he got closer to that end zone I said, "I don't know if he's gonna score." The sideline was going crazy, everybody was jogging down in that situation, and I just remember the pass. I didn't see the catch because [Dolphins LB] Jason Taylor got free and he put a little pressure on [Steelers OL] Max Starks and he got a little bit in my vision so I didn't see the catch right away.

I saw Heath with the ball and I just saw the sideline going crazy. Heath got down and all of a sudden he dove at the last minute, and we were all celebrating because it was a touchdown and we were looking up at the screen and Heath came up and whispered, "I don't know if I got in." He said, "We may want to snap this ball right away." So we ran out and hurried to try and get the extra point team on. Then quickly the snap happened, we kicked the ball and [Dolphins coach] Nick Saban tried to throw his challenge flag at the last minute. He didn't get it in time because he threw it way past the line of scrimmage.

Nobody saw it, we kicked the extra point, and we wound up winning that ball game. For me the thing that stands out was that was the longest touchdown pass in the history of Heinz Field.

Heath was actually my third read on that play. My first read was the fullback in the flat, they ended up taking that lead away, and my next read was to Hines [Ward]. They ended up almost triple teaming Hines, so when they triple teamed him they ended up leaving Heath wide open.

Because they were almost in a two-deep safety look, the backside safety had to cover Cedric Wilson coming in on an in-route. So Heath was wide open, and the backside safety had to run down Heath, and that allowed him to get a head start on that particular play and the safety wasn't able to make it.

We kicked the ball off and on their next drive Joey [Porter] picked off a pass and took it in and we went up and made it a two possession game.

To this day that record stands. I know Ben has thrown 92 yards to Mike Wallace, and 94 to Martavis Bryant, but that's the longest in the history of Heinz Field, and it was to a tight end.

## The Aftermath

The 2006 campaign didn't go as planned for the Steelers. Following their win in Super Bowl XL, the team went .500 in 2006, going 8-8.

Following an offseason horrific motorcycle accident to starting quarterback Ben Roethlisberger, the club struggled to a 2-6 start before turning it around. In what was Bill Cowher's last season, the team went 6-2 in their final eight games of the season to wrap up the year 8-8, knocking the rival Bengals out of the playoffs with a 23-17 win in the final game of the season.

The opener of the season belonged to Batch. Against the Dolphins he went 15-for-25 for 209 yards with three touchdowns and no interceptions and a QB rating of 126.5.

Batch started six games the remainder of his time with the Steelers, with his shining moment coming in 2012 in Week 12 as the team faced a critical test in Baltimore against the Ravens.

The QB stepped in for his second straight start for an injured Ben Roethlisberger and led the team to an emotional 23-20 win as Shaun Suisham kicked a game-winning field goal on the final play.

The lasting image of the win was Batch and Roethlisberger embracing on the sideline, an image that highlighted the closeness of the two QBs and the emotion that Batch felt having a fairly good idea that it would be the last start of his NFL career, which it was.

"At that point I knew that he was coming back the next week, and I knew the way my career had gone—I mean I played so bad the week before against Cleveland, and you kind of anticipate fifteen years—I've been around the business long enough, and you know they are going to try to get younger, and I didn't know if that was going to be my last game starting," Batch said.

Roethlisberger did return the following week, and the team stumbled, losing three of their last four and wrapping up the year at 8-8.

The hug in Baltimore though still ranks as a special moment for Batch, wrapping up a career that saw him be a part of two Super Bowl wins, throw for over 11,000 yards, and win the "Whizzer" White NFL Man of the Year Award in 2012.

"I'm starting my last game in the NFL, and because my moments have come sporadically the last eleven years you don't know when it's going to happen," Batch said.

"At that point we are hugging and yeah I became emotional, I'm thanking him for everything he's done for me, and he's thanking me for everything I've done for him. At that point we're hugging and we're talking, and I'm saying, 'Hey I appreciate everything you've done for me,' and he's saying how much he appreciates me, now let's celebrate."

Batch's post-NFL career has seen him continue working with kids through his "Best of the Batch Foundation," as well as help out a number of other charitable foundations. He also does work on radio and TV in the Pittsburgh area, still talking and giving his opinions about the game he played for fifteen seasons.

# CHAPTER 4

# TUNCH ILKIN

### Offensive Lineman 1980–1992
#### December 31, 1989 vs Houston Oilers at The Astrodome
#### PITTSBURGH STEELERS 23 - HOUSTON OILERS 20 (OT)

Tunch Ilkin was your typical hard-nosed Pittsburgh Steeler who played every down with a sense of purpose. Drafted by the black and gold in sixth round of the 1980 draft, Ilkin played 14 seasons for the Steelers, playing in 177 games. His job was the same week after week, hit the player in front of you harder than you get hit, opening holes for running backs and making sure your quarterback stays upright until he releases the ball.

While you never saw many #62 jerseys on Sunday at Three Rivers Stadium, Ilkin quietly did his job as one of the better offensive linemen year after year on a number of Steelers teams that simply couldn't live up to the dominant teams in the 1970s that took home four Super Bowl titles.

The decline of the organization had to do with the retirement of a number of the stars of the 1970s, along with some forgettable drafts that didn't yield the stars the team needed in order to reload.

Off the field you could tell just by speaking to him that there was a lot more to Ilkin than just your average football player. Always insightful, he took on the role of Steelers' player representative to the NFLPA in 1986, and even served as one of the vice presidents on the NFLPA Executive Committee from 1989 to 1994.

Ilkin was born September 23, 1957, in Istanbul, Turkey. His parents came to the United States when he was two years old, living near Chicago, Illinois. He started to take to football as he grew up, and attended Highland Park High School in Highland Park, Illinois.

## Notes on Tunch Ilkin

| | |
|---|---|
| **Years Played:** | 1980–1992 |
| **Position:** | Offensive Line |
| **Height:** | 6'3" |
| **Weight:** | 263 |
| **Hometown:** | Istanbul, Turkey |
| **Current Residence:** | Pittsburgh, Pennsylvania |
| **Occupation:** | Color Commentator for the Pittsburgh Steelers and broadcaster in Pittsburgh |
| **Accomplishments:** | Ilkin was the sixth-round pick of the Steelers in 1980, 165th pick overall. Started and played on the Steelers offensive line in 131 games from 1984 to his final season with the team in 1992. Played his final season with the Green Bay Packers in 1993. Was a two-time Pro Bowl lineman (1988, 1989). Overall played in 177 games in his NFL career, starting 143 of them. Ilkin served as vice president of the NFL Players Association from 1989 to 1994. He joined the Steelers broadcast booth in 1998, and took over for the retired Myron Cope as color commentator in the 2005 season. |
| **Nickname:** | None |
| **The Game:** | Pittsburgh Steelers vs Houston Oilers in Houston, Texas December 31, 1989 |

He won All Conference and All County honors as a football player, and was given a scholarship in 1975 by Indiana State University. By the time he got to the Steelers in 1980, the glory days of the 1970s faded quickly. Following a win in Super Bowl XIV over the Los Angeles Rams, the Steelers made the playoffs just three more times in coach Chuck Noll's final twelve years on the sideline.

## The Game
*By Tunch Ilkin*

I think a game that sticks out was the 1984 AFC Divisional Game at Denver, but the game that comes to mind even more is 1989 when we beat the Houston Oilers in the wildcard round. We lost to them twice during the regular season, and that was at the time of the Jerry Glanville-Chuck Noll era when both teams really hated each other.

We were down there and the place was going crazy, and there were banners with things like "House of Pain," and the atmosphere was electric. It was one of those hard-fought games, back and forth, and I'll never forget we go into overtime and their running back Lorenzo White took a carry and Rod Woodson strips him of the ball and recovers it.

On our drive after the fumble we actually go 3-and-out, and at first Chuck was going to punt the ball, but then he calls timeout. And I guess the coaches must have talked it over and then they sent Gary Anderson out there and he hits a 50-yard field goal to win it.

I just remember because of the animosity and the bad blood between us and the Oilers, I remember a couple Oilers, Doug Smith, Earl Fuller, Ray Childress, all those guys were on the ground and I remember yelling, "House of Pain, baby! How's it feel?"

That was such a fun game for us, we were lucky to get into the playoffs at all in 1989. We went down to Tampa in the final week of the regular season, and my wife Sharron's family was all down there in Tampa for Christmas, and the deal was we thought by the end of the game we would know if we were in or out of the playoffs, but we didn't.

So I flew home with the team instead of staying down there, and the Monday night game was going to determine if we were in or not. If Cincinnati beat Minnesota than we were out, but if Minnesota beat Cincinnati then we were in.

I remember I was watching that game at my house and they kept showing two homes. They were showing Brian Noble's home—he was a linebacker for Green Bay—and they were showing Dwayne Woodruff's home, and he had a bunch of guys over watching the game. I just remember coming home with the team and thinking, "Either I'm getting on a plane tomorrow if we don't make it or I'm going to practice."

The Monday night game was close, and I remember calling [fellow Steelers OL Craig] "Wolf" [Wolfley] and saying, "Well I guess I'm picking you up," and then saying, "Well it looks like I'm not picking you up." But in the end we made it and got in.

We won another game there in Houston in 1988 on a Sunday night, and that was a great game too, I remember screaming at Robert Lyle, "You'll be watching the playoffs just like us!" But in the end they actually got in it as a wild card.

## The Aftermath

The Steelers 1989 season didn't exactly start out with a lot of promise, as the team lost their first two games by a combined score of 92-10, losing on opening day to the Cleveland Browns 51-0 in the most lopsided loss in franchise history, and then falling 41-10 to the Cincinnati Bengals the following week.

Many referred to the '89 season as the best job of coaching in the Chuck Noll's career. He took a young team that had just lost two games by huge margins, and regrouped them to go 9-5 the rest of the way and get into the playoffs.

"Chuck was great, I remember after the first two games he comes in and grabs a hold of me on that Tuesday, because we were off on Monday and he says to me, 'Keep on smiling Tunch, keep 'em up, keep 'em up.'

"I remember the headline in *USA Today* was like, 'Has the game passed Chuck Noll by?' Since we were 5-11 the year before in 1988 and 0-2 to start 1989, Chuck came into the meeting and he was smiling and when he spoke to the team he said, 'Be careful of what you allow into your brain,' he says to us that your brain is like a swimming pool, and he started to break down the chemicals in a swimming pool, and he starts to see he's losing the room, and then he starts to get frustrated and says, 'In other words, don't let anyone piss in your pool.'"

After the speech, the team made a quick and sudden turnaround that not many saw coming. They beat the Minnesota Vikings at home, and then went to Detroit and beat up the Lions 23-3. Eventually the team sat at 6-7 entering Week 14. The Steelers needed wins in all three of their final games along with some help to reach the postseason, and in the end they made it.

They shut out the New York Jets 13-0, and then dominated the New England Patriots 28-10 at Three Rivers Stadium. Needing a win to even have a chance at the postseason, Pittsburgh beat the Tampa Bay Buccaneers 33-21 in their regular season finale to set up a wild card New Year's Eve game against the Oilers in Houston.

After they upset the Oilers, the team went on the road to take on the AFC's number one seed, the Denver Broncos. They controlled the game in the first half, building a 17-7 lead, but like John Elway usually did back then, he brought the Broncos back for an eventual 24-23 Denver win that ended a memorable Steelers season.

As for Ilkin, he continued with the Steelers into the Bill Cowher era in 1992 before leaving the team to play one year for the Green Bay Packers in 1993. After retiring, he entered the world of the media as well as ministry.

He spent the 1995 season working with NBC. In 1998, he moved officially to the Steelers radio booth, eventually taking the spot of the legendary Myron Cope as the Steelers color man alongside broadcaster Bill Hillgrove for all Steelers game across their radio network.

His work not only continues with the Steelers, but in ministry, as since his conversion from Islam to being a Christian, Ilkin has been busy sharing his love of Christ with others. He has helped in and served in youth ministry, sports ministry, and today serves as the Director of Men's Ministries for South Hills Bible Chapel.

"I thank God every day for my thirty-five years here in Pittsburgh. Number one the greatest thing that happened to me is when I found Christ," Ilkin said. "As a former drug user and thief, it was a very dark past, and then I met a bunch of guys who love Jesus, and loved each other, and loved me and shared with me the good news of the gospel. That was the greatest thing that happened to me here."

# CHAPTER 5

# RAMON FOSTER

**Offensive Lineman 2009–Present**

**January 15, 2011 vs Baltimore Ravens at Heinz Field**

**PITTSBURGH STEELERS 31 - BALTIMORE RAVENS 24**

When it comes to protecting Pittsburgh Steelers franchise quarterback Ben Roethlisberger, undrafted free agent Ramon Foster has been a gem for the organization since joining them in 2009.

Nicknamed "The Big Ragu," Foster played 44 games in college, and was All-SEC in his freshman and junior seasons at the University of Tennessee.

He was able to make an impact upon joining the Steelers, and the last three seasons has started every game that he's played in.

"The organization as a whole, there's nothing but positive out of it," Foster said. "The way the Rooneys go about it, letting the coaches be coaches, the way they do things behind the scenes, it's been great.

"They know players' faces, they know players' names, and they are very welcoming. That's one big thing that I like about it."

Foster has brought into the way that the Steelers do business, the fact that every season there are high expectations for the black and gold—championship expectations.

AP Photo/ Don Wright

## Notes on Ramon Foster

| | |
|---|---|
| **Years Played:** | 2009–Present |
| **Position:** | Offensive Line |
| **Height:** | 6'6" |
| **Weight:** | 325 |
| **Hometown:** | Henning, Tennessee |
| **Current Residence:** | Pittsburgh, Pennsylvania |
| **Occupation:** | Offensive Lineman for the Pittsburgh Steelers |
| **Accomplishments:** | Signed by the Steelers as an undrafted free agent in April of 2009, and since has started 57 of 72 games. Was a three-year starter in basketball at Ripley High School in Ripley, TN, and also was part of the track and field team, putting up a career-best shot put of 45–11. Played his college ball at Tennessee, and upon being drafted by the Steelers made his first start on November 29, 2009, against the rival Baltimore Ravens. Started 59 games over the last four seasons with the black and gold. In the 2014 offseason Foster attended the NFL Sports Journalism & Communication Boot Camp, and will contribute to the teams' official website during the season. |
| **Nickname:** | None |
| **The Game:** | Pittsburgh Steelers vs Baltimore Ravens in Pittsburgh, Pennsylvania January 15, 2011 |

He got a taste of it in 2010 when the team made it to Super Bowl XLV before falling to the Green Bay Packers, and again in 2011 when they made the playoffs before falling in a wild card upset to Tim Tebow and the Denver Broncos 29-23 in a gut-wrenching loss that stunned the franchise.

"We're expected to win, and when we don't it's a surprise. I think a lot of the teams their goal is to make the playoffs. Ours is to win the Super Bowl—every year. You go into every season thinking Super Bowl or nothing," Foster said.

Playing a position that is always in need, the guard knows that his role is to stay out of the spotlight, and to open holes for running backs like Le'Veon Bell and keep his QB on his feet while he looks downfield to throw.

There is a precedent with the Steelers under head coach Mike Tomlin, one that has the team looking to play at a high level every week, and one that makes the team prepare knowing other teams are going to raise their level to play them.

"I'm not quite sure if it was Coach Tomlin or who came up with the saying, 'The Standard is The Standard,' but that saying is very true when you are dealing with the Steelers," Foster said.

"I think other teams know that, when other teams play us, it's not the same team we see on film, in my opinion they seem to play us harder."

Foster got that feeling first hand when the team won the AFC Title in 2010. The first test was a third meeting with their most heated rivals, the Baltimore Ravens, a team that was hungry as they came into Heinz Field for an AFC Divisional showdown on January 15, 2011.

# The Game

*By Ramon Foster*

In 2010 we were on a Super Bowl run, and in the AFC Divisional Game we played Baltimore first, it was our third time playing Baltimore.

It's funny that entire season I don't think for a second we thought we were going to lose any of those games leading into the playoffs.

We got a first round bye after we went 12-4, and that Baltimore game, it was a game for the ages in my opinion.

We knew we could go up and play with anybody, and we knew we could beat anybody.

Simply put, it was us against them. Anyone that knows that series or that game knows that it's always a big game and this time it was for even bigger stakes because it was to make it to the AFC Championship.

We were down in that game for the most part, we trailed 21-7 at the half, but it just seemed like with the year that guys were having, we knew we could come back.

The lead that Baltimore had in that game, it was one of those things where we felt we could overcome it despite trailing by 14. We had done it that season before.

Ben [Roethlisberger] had just a great year, and we were playing well up front on the line, and in general guys played so well it was the type of season that we felt no one could stop us.

We had high goals coming into the season. In games we always wanted to go out and score on first drives, and we were doing that.

The turning point in that game for me was when we had a fumble, and their defensive end, Cory Redding, picked it up and ran it in for a touchdown late in the first quarter to put us down 14-7.

We were backed up on our end of the field, when they ruled it a fumble and they scored.

It was crazy, I walked right past the ball and could have picked it up. That was one time I wished I would have just picked up the ball and run with it.

At the time we all thought we had heard whistles, and no one was circling around the ball or anything, so we didn't even realize that there was a Baltimore player running with the ball into the end zone.

We went to the sidelines, surprised at what happened, and we just turned it on from there, and we ended up winning the game late 31-24 to get to the AFC Championship Game.

The catch that Antonio Brown made on our final drive to put us in a position to win that game, it really put his career on a great path, that was one of the greatest catches I've seen.

He's made a lot more, but the situation that we were in, I don't think you can ask for a better catch.

We went in and scored from there, and I think that they knew after that it was going to be our night after that catch by Antonio and score.

It was one of the best comebacks I've ever been a part of based on the situation we were in, and just beating them in the playoffs was a great year and a great game for us.

## The Aftermath

The win over the Ravens advanced the Steelers to the AFC Championship Game the following Sunday.

The opponent was a surprise, as most felt they would be taking on the 14-win New England Patriots, a team that had won eight straight entering the postseason, and owned the NFL's best offense, scoring 32.4 points a game.

The opposition for New England in their first playoff game in Foxboro was a rival, the New York Jets: a team with a lot of bark, a solid defense, and a coach in Rex Ryan who wasn't afraid to speak his mind.

The Jets went into the Patriots home and pulled off a major upset. Coming in as 9.5-point underdogs, the Jets beat the Patriots 28-21 to advance to play the Steelers the following week at Heinz Field for the right to advance to Super Bowl XLV.

Foster was well aware of the Jets and how well they were playing when they beat New England to advance to play the Steelers.

"We knew we were going to play our best game, the Jets were red hot and had one of the craziest defenses that I had ever seen," Foster said.

"The Jets had beaten the Patriots, and I remember distinctly Bart Scott had come out and during his post-game interview the reporter asked him, 'Are you ready to go to Pittsburgh?' and he gave his famous quote, 'Can't wait.'"

"We knew we were going to have to be on our Ps and Qs. You look at the Jets defense and they will have just two defensive linemen in and a crazy amount of linebackers and defensive backs and will try to confuse you."

Unlike the week before when the Jets took an 11-point lead early over the Patriots, the Steelers offensive line dominated early, putting together a nine-minute drive to start the game to take a 7-0 lead.

The barrage of scoring continued for the Steelers, as they scored 24 unanswered points, including a defensive touchdown by William Gay, until the Jets finally scored a field goal to end the first half.

"We picked it up early in the game and we scored as we needed to. We didn't even score any points in the second half at all, we did enough in the first half to actually get that done."

New York closed the game to 24-19 and Steelers Nation was biting off every inch of finger nails they had left before a critical third-down conversion with two minutes to go clinched the win.

With the Steelers facing a third-and-six, Ben Roethlisberger and the team took a huge risk, rolling out and hitting Antonio Brown with a pass for 14 yards which ended any hope the Jets had.

While it wasn't a pretty win by any means, it was a victory that put the Steelers a game away from their seventh championship, and one that Foster still recalls with great fondness.

"I remember myself at the end of the game on the field doing the Jets celebration where you throw your hands out like a plane while we were on the field.

"Being on the stage and getting the AFC Championship hat and shirt it's one of the best things ever," Foster said.

Two weeks after the win over the Jets, the Steelers took the biggest stage in football, playing the Green Bay Packers in Dallas in Super Bowl XLV.

Pittsburgh fell behind in the game 21-3, and while they rallied to close the game to 31-25 with the ball with two minutes left, the Packers defense held and the Steelers left Dallas without a title.

"It would have been nice to cap off that season with the Super Bowl, but it just didn't work out in our favor," Foster recalls.

The guard has been a staple in the Steelers offense, playing and starting in every game from 2012 on for the black and gold.

While there's still that hunger for a seventh title for the Steelers, Foster has great memories of the playoff run of 2010 that fell just short of a championship.

"Those last three games of that season—[that] was as excited as I have ever been playing in a game before," Foster said.

# CHAPTER 6

# DERMONTTI DAWSON

### Center 1988–2000

**October 14, 1991 vs New York Giants at Three Rivers Stadium**

**NEW YORK GIANTS 23 - PITTSBURGH STEELERS 20**

Playing center in Pittsburgh has never been an easy job. The bar was raised to an incredibly high level in the 1970s by Hall of Famer Mike Webster, who owned the position better than anyone in the game, and before that Ray Mansfield was a staple at the center spot for the Steelers' first two Super Bowl titles.

When it came time for the Steelers to look ahead at who was going to take over for Webster, they saw his hopeful replacement in a quiet leader named Dermontti Dawson, from the University of Kentucky. Taken in the second round in 1988, Dawson came in and had the opportunity to learn under Webster, as he lined up next to him at guard his rookie season, all the while taking notes about the position that would be eventually be his.

In 1989, Webster moved on to Kansas City, and the center position was Dawson's. It was a transition that not only saw the position stay as good as it was under Webster, but actually may have been even better.

Dawson played thirteen seasons with the Steelers, and was one of the best players at the center position in the history of the game.

AP Photo/Gene J. Puskar

# Notes on Dermontti Dawson

| | |
|---|---|
| **Years Played:** | 1988–2000 |
| **Position:** | Center |
| **Height:** | 6'2" |
| **Weight:** | 288 |
| **Hometown:** | Lexington, Kentucky |
| **Current Residence:** | San Diego, California |
| **Occupation:** | Sales Executive for promotional products company |
| **Accomplishments:** | Seven-time Pro Bowl and six-time All-Pro selection at the center position in his thirteen seasons with the Steelers. Was the Steelers second-round pick, 44th pick overall in the 1988 NFL Draft. Took over the center spot for Hall of Famer Mike Webster to start the 1989 season. Played both center and guard at Kentucky, and lettered all four seasons at the University. Played in 170 games straight for the Steelers, second most in team history. In 1993, he was named co-AFC Offensive Lineman of the Year by the NFLPA and in 1996 he was named the NFL Alumni's Offensive Lineman of the Year. Dawson took home the title of first-team center on the NFL's 1990 All-Decade Team. Also was named to the Steelers All-Time Team in 2007 as the franchise's 75th season celebration. |
| **Nickname:** | "Dirt" & "Ned Flanders" |
| **The Game:** | Pittsburgh Steelers vs New York Giants in Pittsburgh, Pennsylvania October 14, 1991 |

He called the blocking assignments and made sure whoever was running the ball would have a hole, and whoever went back to pass had protection up the middle.

Dawson's teammates nicknamed him "Ned Flanders" a character from the hit TV show *The Simpsons*. The reason why was simple: he was always the nicest guy on the field, a player who always led by example, and never complained, despite at times having to take on two or even three blockers at a time.

In 2012 Dawson was given the highest honor for a player, as he was named to the Pro Football Hall of Fame in Canton, Ohio. Just like when he was on the field, he was humble and gracious when talking about being alongside the greats in the history of the game.

# The Game

*By Dermontti Dawson*

The game that stood out to me, it was the 1991 season and it was a Monday night game against the New York Giants.

I had to go back and think about what game I had that was a pretty good game that I got comments from the coaches that I played my ass off, and it was this game.

The game was in Pittsburgh at Three Rivers Stadium, and we lost the game 23-20.

We always went to the hotel the night before games, and usually the day of the game we had time to go home before the game, and then we come back to the hotel.

Once we get together at the hotel we have meetings and go over the game plan, and then we head on over to the stadium to get ready for the game and we go through all our pregame stuff.

When I got up that Sunday morning I was sick as a dog. I came to find out that I came down with the flu. How I came down with that I have no idea, but I was completely exhausted.

Once I got to hotel I went down to the trainer's room and talked to those guys and I told them, "Hey, I'm really sick." So they told me, "Go back up to your room and get into bed." So I went back upstairs and slept in my room for I'm not sure how many hours, and then I got up for the pregame meal, but I didn't have too much of an appetite.

We all went to the stadium for pregame, and they went ahead and gave me an IV to try and hydrate me a little bit.

I had my pants on, but I didn't even go out for pregame warmups. I just stayed in the trainer's office and slept until it was time to go out for the start of the game.

I went out, played the game, and of course I had zero energy throughout the course of the game. You know what it's like when you have the flu and you just feel totally exhausted and you're laboring with your breathing.

Still though, I was able to endure the first half, played a phenomenal game, came back in and they gave me another IV, and played the second half.

I was completely exhausted after the game. We fought but in the end we lost.

Even the coaches on Tuesday when we looked at film, they said, "You played a hell of a game, you played your ass off." Our position coaches: our offensive line coach Ron Blackledge and the coordinators, Tom Moore, our offensive coordinator; they talked about how well I played, even with the flu. They said, "You couldn't tell anything was wrong with you." We had that trapping scheme of offense, and they had two good middle linebackers in Pepper Johnson and Gary Reasons. They were still a really good defense in 1991.

I recall this one draw play that we ran, L.T. (Lawrence Taylor) was lined up on the left hand side, he came around John Jackson, who was our tackle, and John had done a pretty good job on him.

Taylor comes around and then ran down the middle of the field and he was the first one to make the tackle of our running back, Barry Foster. That guy was just unbelievable.

We looked at it later on film and I said, "My goodness that guy ran all the way around our tackle and then pursued and was the first one to make the tackle from behind." Of course Barry on the play was cutting and everything else, but I just remember vividly on that play on the tape when we were looking at the film. I couldn't believe it.

That was one of my most memorable games.

## The Aftermath

The 1991 season for the Steelers was filled with frustration and near misses. The team was inconsistent, going 7-9 in what turned out to be Chuck Noll's final season.

The team suffered a four-game losing streak after starting 3-2, basically putting them out of the playoff race as they sat at 3-6 going into Week 10. They lost a tough game in Cleveland in Week 8 to the Browns 17-14, and in Week 9 they had a shot in the final minute but failed in a tough 20-13 loss in Denver to the Broncos.

They won four of their final seven games, including their last two to end the season two games under .500.

The Week 7, three-point loss to the Giants was a snapshot of just how up and down the 1991 Steelers were.

The Steelers fell behind 20-0 to the defending Super Bowl champions before clawing back to score 20 points in just over eighteen minutes to tie the game up with fifty seconds left.

Instead of riding that momentum to a win, the Steelers defense allowed the Giants to drive down the field to allow Giants kicker Matt Bahr the chance to kick a 44-yard field goal to win the game 23-20 as time expired.

The loss put the Steelers in a tailspin, and despite the strong play of Dawson, who went to play in seven Pro Bowls and was a six-time Pro Bowl selection, the team lost four straight and didn't win another game until Week 11 in Cincinnati.

Dawson was part of the team's rebirth in 1992 when Bill Cowher came aboard, and helped running back Barry Foster set a single-season franchise record with 1,692 rushing yards.

The Steelers were built on power and speed on the offensive line, and with Dawson leading the way the team always seemed to be at or near the top when it came to running the football.

Dawson was named to the 1990s NFL All Decade Team, and in 2007 was named to the Steelers All-Time Team as part of the franchise's 75th anniversary.

There was no doubt that Dawson was more than a suitable replacement for Mike Webster when he left the team in 1989, and many in the NFL regard Dawson as the all-time best center ever to play the game.

# CHAPTER 7

# LEE FLOWERS

### Safety 1995–2002
### January 14, 1996 vs Indianapolis Colts at Three Rivers Stadium
### PITTSBURGH STEELERS 20 - INDIANAPOLIS COLTS 16

The Pittsburgh Steelers were poised for greatness at the start of the 1995 season.

They still had to deal with the bitter taste of a crushing 17-13 home AFC Championship Game loss in January 1995 to the San Diego Chargers, but had high hopes of a return to the postseason and this time the ability to get the job done.

That offseason the team drafted a safety out of Georgia Tech named Lee Flowers, a hard-hitting defensive back who wound up playing eight seasons in Pittsburgh, eventually becoming the anchor of a defense in transition.

He came in at a time when the Steelers were talking Super Bowl, but still needed to add youth to a team that seemed to always lose a few players due to free agency.

Flowers fit the mold of a player who was young, hungry, and willing to learn. He got to know the Steelers quickly upon being drafted, and one person that made quite an impression on him was one who at first he didn't recognize.

"On a personal level, Mr. Rooney shook hands with everybody in the locker room. I remember my rookie year, about six games into it,

I was always wondering, 'Who was this little guy walking around shaking people's hands?'" Flowers said.

"I didn't know, and come to find out that was the owner of the team. I thought that was very important to a lot of the players in the locker room."

Flowers had the benefit of learning from some of the best players in the game. He had a Hall-of-Fame cornerback in Rod Woodson in the same locker room, as well as defensive stars like Greg Lloyd and Kevin Greene, as well as fellow safety Carnell Lake.

The 1995 team also leaned heavily on the leadership of its head coach, Bill Cowher. In just his third season as coach, Cowher had raised the bar high, with already two AFC Central Titles and a trip to the AFC Championship Game in 1994.

"Coach Cowher always kept us level headed, he never really panicked and always stayed within his personality," Flowers said.

"Then to add we had a lot of good veterans, Rod Woodson, Carnell Lake, Greg Lloyd, Neil O'Donnell, a lot of guys who had been there, and had been in certain situations.

"We also had a lot of rookies who really paid attention to the game. We had a good mixture of guys that year, and I think that's what made me the player I was."

That's not to say that it all came easy for the 1995 Steelers. They lost Woodson to a torn ACL on opening day in a win over the Detroit Lions, an injury that forced him to miss the rest of the regular season and the first two playoff games.

They also lost their quarterback, Neil O'Donnell, to a broken finger that would keep him on the sidelines for the first few weeks following their opening day win.

The team slumped, maybe due to the pressure of being picked by many to represent the AFC in Super Bowl XXX, or maybe combined with the injuries, the club found themselves 3-4 after seven games, and some felt the season was on life support.

"I remember we were 3-4, and we had a 'players only meeting,' and at the time a number of players stood up and talked, we had to cut back on some things in the locker room," Flowers recalls.

AP Photo/Chris Gardner

# Notes on Lee Flowers

| | |
|---|---|
| **Years Played:** | 1995–2002 |
| **Position:** | Safety |
| **Height:** | 6'0" |
| **Weight:** | 213 |
| **Hometown:** | Columbia, South Carolina |
| **Current Residence:** | Atlanta, Georgia |
| **Occupation:** | Works for a residential construction company |
| **Accomplishments:** | Drafted in the fifth round of the 1995 draft, and played mostly on special teams his rookie year as the team won the AFC Championship and played in Super Bowl XXX in a losing effort to the Dallas Cowboys. Took over at safety for Carnell Lake after cornerback Chad Scott suffered an injury in 1998 and then coach Bill Cowher moved Lake to corner and Flowers to safety. He started in seventy-five games over the next five seasons with the Steelers, recording four interceptions and forcing eight fumbles during that time. Ended his career starting 75 of 112 games, recording 306 tackles. Left the team following the 2002 season and signed with the Denver Broncos, but never played a down in Denver. |
| **Nickname:** | None |
| **The Game:** | Pittsburgh Steelers vs Indianapolis Colts in Pittsburgh, Pennsylvania |
| | January 14, 1996 |

"No video game playing, no cell phones, intangible things that helped us out and helped us to re-focus. Myself being a rookie, I didn't know the magnitude of how everybody felt the previous year because I wasn't there.

"A lot of guys talked about how we just couldn't go down this same road again. We needed to do something to turn that season around and get our footing under us again."

The team rallied, starting with a home win over the Jacksonville Jaguars, and then a key overtime road win the following week over the Chicago Bears.

The team wound up winning eight of their last nine, losing a meaningless final game in Green Bay to the Packers, a game it would have won if not for a dropped pass in the end zone in the final seconds by Yancey Thigpen.

"I go back to Coach Cowher, that following week after we were 3-4, he came in and told us, 'Don't peak too early,' that was always his motto," Flowers said.

"After that we ripped off eight games in a row, then we lost our last game before the playoffs. At that point though everything really started to fall in place for us."

The team entered the playoffs as the number two seed, and following a 40-21 win over the Buffalo Bills in the AFC Divisional Playoff Game, the team waited to see who they would face in the AFC Championship Game.

Enter the Indianapolis Colts—an upstart team who got into the playoffs as a wild card with a 9-7 record. Led by a gutsy quarterback in Jim Harbaugh, they sailed past the defending AFC Champions in San Diego with a 35-20 win in the wild card game.

In the AFC Divisional Playoff Game, the Colts were eight-point underdogs, but again outplayed the Kansas City Chiefs, led by Steelers coach Bill Cowher's mentor, Marty Schottenheimer.

The Chiefs committed four turnovers, and kicker Lin Elliott missed three field goals. The Colts pulled out a 10-7 win to advance to the AFC Championship Game and a showdown in Pittsburgh.

Upon the Colts' winning, Steeler fans celebrated, as they felt a home game against a wild card team meant they might as well start making plans for Super Bowl XXX.

"You even look at Indianapolis when they came into Pittsburgh, nobody gave them a chance to beat Kansas City in Kansas City the week before," Flowers said.

"Kansas City was 13-3 in the regular season, and I remember when Indianapolis went into Arrowhead Stadium and won that game, you could stick your head outside in the city of Pittsburgh and hear everybody screaming because we knew we had another home playoff game."

The 1995 AFC Championship Game was a classic, a game that to this day is remembered fondly by Steelers fans as one of high drama, with the team trying to exercise the demons of its AFC Title Game loss to San Diego the season before.

# The Game
*By Lee Flowers*

I remember every game, I think as a player it's always a once-in-a-lifetime moment. The way we prepared, we really studied our tails off getting ready the week of the game.

For me, the biggest game I remember was the 1995 AFC Championship Game when we played Indianapolis.

I wasn't a starter at the time, but that game in itself really made me appreciate what the Steelers were all about.

The atmosphere in the air, you could just feel the fans, you could feel everybody's heart beating in that stadium during that game, especially in the fourth quarter when we got behind and then during the "Hail Mary" by Indianapolis on the final play.

For me, I had a couple special team's tackles in that game, and that shot my career forward a little for being a special team's player and eventually to be a starter.

It was just a great atmosphere, and it showed really what Pittsburgh was about. Not just the team, but the city. We never give up, we keep on fighting, and we're going to punch you in the mouth till the final bell rings.

It was a great game, and now you look at where all these guys from that game are at today, a number are in the Hall of Fame.

Jim Harbaugh, the quarterback that day for the Colts, went through San Francisco and now he's the coach at Michigan.

There was just a lot of big names in that game and I think people forget about that.

I think that game really catapulted Pittsburgh to where they are now, it was a game of resiliency and never giving up and just fighting to the end.

We had so many good players at that time, potentially five Hall of Fame players in that game for us.

For being a rookie from Georgia Tech in my first year to going to the Super Bowl, you really couldn't write the script any better.

Obviously if we would have won the Super Bowl that would have been great, but really as a player that's the game that stands out to me.

Even when we got behind in the fourth quarter after Harbaugh threw a long touchdown pass to Floyd Turner, Coach Cowher always did a great job having each unit control their respective players.

Our special teams coach kept us calm, the defensive coaches kept players calm, as did the offensive coaches.

As a head coach you're indicative of what type of coaching staff you have, and Coach Cowher's demeanor was fiery, but he knew when to step back and say, "Look guys, let's concentrate. Let's focus, because we can beat this team. We are better than this team." When you look back at what brought us to that game, all the things that we went through, the adversity that we went through just to make it to that game.

We put our whole season together for a couple of plays and just all three units were able to make some plays. In the end it came down to that "Hail Mary" which our cornerback Randy Fuller knocked down that allowed us to win the game.

I do recall, though, even when we got behind in the fourth quarter, there wasn't a lot of stress on our sideline. I think when you start to stress and start to panic you go out and play like that.

We just stayed calm and did what we knew how to do. We knew we were physically better than them, and I think they knew it.

We never panicked. We just stayed calm and let our actions speak for themselves.

Once we got the lead we made a big play on the following kickoff, stopping them deep in their own territory.

That was a big play, as I think our job as special team players was to get the crowd on their feet. We knew we could change the atmosphere in that stadium and in that game one way or another.

If we let a guy run a kickoff or a punt back, as they say in basketball, you could feel the momentum change.

We always felt like we controlled the momentum on special teams. You look at the players that were on special teams that year and most of us went on to start either for the Steelers or elsewhere in the NFL.

We just felt like we could control the tempo of the game and we knew we needed to get the crowd into the game and that was our best access to do it, on that kickoff.

At the time Fred McAfee was the captain of the special teams, and he went out there and did what he was supposed to do, and made a huge play.

They were driving down the field, and the crowd was super into it during those final minutes. They got to our 29-yard line with five seconds left. It all came down to that last play.

I was praying for that "Hail Mary" to get knocked down, intercept the ball or whatever, just as long as they didn't catch it.

We were able to come up with a play and get the win. It was a great feeling knowing we were headed to the Super Bowl.

That was a special year for me.

## The Aftermath

Super Bowl XXX was the third championship meeting between the Steelers and Dallas Cowboys. The Cowboys were heavy favorites, and it appeared early on those that felt it would be another NFC blowout were going to be right.

Dallas jumped out to a 13-0 lead before the Steelers rallied for a touchdown right before half to close it to 13-7 as Thigpen pulled in a score on a perfect slant in front of future Hall of Fame cornerback Deion Sanders.

That's when things for the Steelers took a turn. Their reliable quarterback, Neil O'Donnell, who had thrown just seven interceptions all season, threw three in the second half, two of which directly to Dallas touchdowns.

"I think that's what hurt so many guys in the locker room to witness that on the field," Flowers said of O'Donnell's interceptions.

The Steelers controlled the second half of the game, holding down the high-powered Dallas offense led by Hall of Fame quarterback Troy Aikman and Hall of Fame running back Emmitt Smith.

Flowers recalls the week leading up to the game, and just how the Steelers were ready for whatever the Cowboys were bringing with them.

"The whole week practice was great, the atmosphere was great, we were focused, and Dallas had to deal with all their media and we were the underdogs," Flowers recalls. "We didn't have to deal with all that nonsense."

Then once halftime ended, the Steelers defense dominated, harassing Aikman and holding Smith to just eight yards over the final thirty minutes.

"We had them beat up and down the field. The way Neil played in the AFC Championship Game we thought we were going to go in there and beat Dallas by two touchdowns," Flowers said.

It was not meant to be, as the two crushing interceptions were too much to overcome, as Larry Brown took home the MVP for two picks of O'Donnell.

"Certain things just stick with you for life and that's something that will stick with me the rest of my life," Flowers said.

"It was a great experience and how many guys can say they went to the Super Bowl their rookie year?"

Flowers' career was just starting, and finally in 1998 he became a starter in the Steelers defensive backfield.

His best season came in 2002, when he picked off three passes, recovered a fumble, and had four sacks before retiring from the NFL after the season.

# CHAPTER 8

# JEFF REED

**Kicker 2002–2010**

**December 1, 2002 vs Jacksonville Jaguars at Alltel Stadium**

**PITTSBURGH STEELERS 25 - JACKSONVILLE JAGUARS 23**

Kickers tend to march to beat of their own drums, and one former Steelers kicker who lived that phrase more than any other was Jeff Reed.

The Kansas City, Missouri, native kicked parts of nine seasons with the Steelers, earning two Super Bowl rings as the team's kicker during the 2005 and 2008 seasons as they won Super Bowls XL and XLIII.

Reed earned his keep with the black and gold, as he's the second-highest scoring Steeler in franchise history, with 733 points. He trails only longtime kicker Gary Anderson's franchise mark of 1,343 points.

He also became a fan favorite for his platinum-dyed hair and quirky personality, enjoying the company of fans when attending and cheering on the NHL's Pittsburgh Penguins.

Reed was as good as any kicker in the NFL during the two playoff seasons in which the Steelers won Super Bowls, going 8-for-8 in those two post seasons.

He had one of his best seasons in 2009, going 27-for-31. His efficiency dropped off in 2010, which eventually led to his release.

The kicker had many memorable moments with the Steelers, and will always be remembered as one of the clutch kickers in the history of the franchise.

AP Photo/ Tom E. Puskar

## Notes on Jeff Reed

| | |
|---|---|
| **Years Played:** | 2002–2010 |
| **Position:** | Kicker |
| **Height:** | 5'11" |
| **Weight:** | 225 |
| **Hometown:** | Kansas City, Missouri |
| **Current Residence:** | Charlotte, North Carolina |
| **Occupation:** | Broadcaster and Podcast Host |
| **Accomplishments:** | Reed graduated ninth in his class out of 365 at Mecklenburg High School in Charlotte, NC. Was involved in National Honor Society in high school. Was an honorable mention All-ACC pick as a senior and a second-team All-ACC player as a junior at North Carolina. Was undrafted in 2002, but joined the Steelers following an injury to kicker Todd Peterson, and earned a pair of Super Bowl rings with the Steelers, winning titles with the club in 2005 and 2008. Ranks second all-time in points with the Steelers with 919 points, trailing only Gary Anderson. Kicked 307 PATs and 204 field goals in Steelers career. Was 23-for-25 in field goals in 2007 (92 percent) which ranks third all-time in field goal percentage for a single season with the Steelers. Is the second-most accurate in team history, ranking twelfth in NFL history with an 81.9 percent accuracy rate (204 of 249). |
| **Nickname:** | None |
| **The Game:** | Pittsburgh Steelers vs Jacksonville Jaguars in Jacksonville, Florida December 1, 2002 |

# The Game

*By Jeff Reed*

It's easy to say the coolest game of your career is the Super Bowl because that's why you play the game, but for me the first Super Bowl, besides the fact that we won and I had the opening kickoff and all the flashes, that game was pretty boring, as a fan or as a player.

The second Super Bowl [XLIII] will always be one of the best ever, because I thought we were going to kill Arizona and we were, but all the sudden we lost our mojo, then we scored and I contributed.

I also have the shortest field goal in Super Bowl history, it's at least a record of some kind. It was 18 yards, on the first drive of the game. We wanted to go for it, but we took the points.

Those are great, but if I had to pull out a game, it would have to be 2002, my second career game ever. In Jacksonville. I was 6-for-6 on field goals, and I had 19 points and we won 25-23.

The reason that was so cool is, yeah, it was great to make all those kicks, it was kind of a breakthrough like, "Yeah, this guy's actually good" kind of thing, and that was great, but it was more of the fact that just weeks before that I tried out for Jacksonville, and I outkicked all the guys they brought in.

Tom Coughlin [Jaguars head coach] was there, and I will never forget him, how rude he was. Things change over the years but that's how I remember him.

I went 14-for-15 on the tryout. Every kick was a touchback on the kickoffs. I missed a 45 or a 47 yarder. That's the only one I missed, and the other three guys, actually no one kicked badly, but I kicked the best.

He sat down with each one of us, they ended up picking Richie Cunningham, who was only there for a couple of weeks and after that never kicked again. Coughlin told me, "You were pretty consistent, but you're also a rookie and we don't know if we can take a shot on you. You missed one." To me I was like, "14-for-15 if I am a coach, if I'm a kicker, if I'm the one with the stats I'll take it." 14-for-15 is 90 percent, I don't know what the problem is, but I didn't say anything, I was just a young guy trying to break in, and I said, "All right, thanks for the tryout." Then I got a chance to try out for Pittsburgh and that was a wild tryout. Nonetheless, I got the job somehow and we went to Jacksonville the second week. That's when I made those field goals.

Seeing his face and his curse words under his breath, after you watch the highlights you say to yourself, "You know what—karma sucks." It was a great feeling, other than having all the points and everyone saying I'm the hero, blah, blah, blah. It was a cool feeling to know in life, sometimes you have to take a chance on someone to see what they are made of.

That's anything from relationships, to coaches, to players, to your bucket-list items, to whatever it may be. That's why I learned from that and I thought it was really cool.

To see his face it was kind of like, "I told you so." Of course not me taking all the credit, the guys that held for me, Tommy Maddox and all the guys that contributed to the game and I was just out there kicking doing my thing, that was a memorable game.

Just weeks before that, I had a bad tryout in New York with the Giants, and they told me if I had a great tryout I would be their kicker the opening night Thursday night and this was Monday before the season opened. And I didn't kick very well to be honest and they said I would never kick in this league.

It was kind of one of those things, even though I was on the Steelers, and I had a good opening game and then I went to Jacksonville and did that, it was kind of like a huge confidence booster for me, telling me I can do anything I put my mind to.

Todd Peterson was the kicker there, and he broke a rib and he was 12-for-22 before he broke his rib so they were kind of looking for a reason to replace him, and then he got hurt so it was easier. I tried out with Michael Husted, Joe O'Donnell, myself, and this kid named Danny Boyd.

I hit the longest field goal, but nobody stood out as far as one guy being the best. The Rooneys, Coach Cowher, scouts, everybody was out there. It was sleeting, high school uprights, the awesome mud that we played on the first few years of my career—it was all that.

I had never kicked in that stuff. I thought 50 degrees was cold. You kind of hit reality with that. There were guys falling down, begging for another opportunity, Coach Cowher was laughing at them. I was laughing because I didn't have the right shoes; I wasn't prepared to kick in weather like that.

It was just an opportunity that I hoped and prayed went my way. And if it didn't, then man, I learned something. It did go my way, but it wasn't like I stood out. I think my character stood out, and that's why [GM] Kevin [Colbert] and Coach Cowher took a chance on me.

They saw something in me. I think it was more about my character and they said, "You know what, if a guy is going to learn how to kick as a rookie, this is the hardest place to do it, so we'll see what he's made of."

## The Aftermath

The key Week 13 win for the Steelers over the Jaguars with Reed leading the way put the team at 7-4-1 on the season.

The club wound up the season 10-5-1, good enough to win the first ever AFC North Title. The team won a memorable shootout with the Cleveland Browns in the wild card round, rallying from a 24-7 third-quarter deficit to pull out a last-second 36-33 win.

The following week the dream of a Super Bowl birth ended in the divisional round as the team fell to the Tennessee Titans 34-31 in overtime.

For eight seasons from 2003 to 2010, Reed went over the 100-point mark as the team's field goal and extra point kicker.

His best season point-wise was 2004 when he hit for 28 field goals and a total of 124 points.

Reed held the kicking job with the Steelers longer than any other kicker since Anderson, staying in the position for parts of nine seasons before his eventual release after struggling in 2010.

Coming off an excellent 2009 in which he missed just four field goals the whole season, Reed was 15-for-22 in field goals in 2010, including missing all four kicks between 40 to 49 yards before he was let go in November of that season.

Reed's best day of his career was that second career game in Jacksonville in 2002, as he never again kicked six field goals in a single game.

On January 2, 2005, he went 5-for-5 in field goals in a win over the Bills, and five other times in his NFL career he hit for four field goals in a game.

The final four-field-goal game of his career came after his release from the Steelers, as Reed joined the San Francisco 49ers in December of 2010 for injured kicker Joe Nedney. In a 40-21 win over the Seattle Seahawks, Reed hit for four extra points and four field goals.

# CHAPTER 9

# MIKE TOMCZAK

**Quarterback 1993–1999**
**October 7, 1996 vs Kansas City Chiefs at Arrowhead Stadium**
**PITTSBURGH STEELERS 17-KANSAS CITY CHIEFS 7**

Mike Tomczak spent seven seasons with the Pittsburgh Steelers, but most fans seem to remember only one of those years: 1996 when he started fifteen games including two playoffs games while leading the Steelers to the AFC Central Title.

The Calumet City, Illinois, native came to the Steelers after tenures with the Chicago Bears, and two one-year stays with the Green Bay Packers and the rival Cleveland Browns. It was that 1992 season with the Browns that the Steelers coaching staff got an up-close look at Tomczak, as he beat Bill Cowher's upstart team in a Week 5 game in Cleveland 17-9.

While Tomczak's numbers didn't overwhelm that day (10-for-17 for 171 yards and a touchdown) they were good enough to entice the Steelers to talk to him that offseason, and eventually ink him as the backup to then starting quarterback Neil O'Donnell. "There was a chemistry there that Bill Cowher and the organization had a strong imprint of success, obviously prior to those years with Chuck Noll and everything that was pretty well documented."

AP Photo/Ed Zurga

# Notes on Mike Tomczak

**Years Played:** 1993–1999
**Position:** Quarterback
**Height:** 6'1"
**Weight:** 210
**Hometown:** Calumet City, Illinois
**Current Residence:** Pittsburgh, Pennsylvania
**Occupation:** President of the Esmark High School "All-American" recognition program
**Accomplishments:** Graduated from OSU with a major in Communication. Undrafted out of Ohio State, signed with the Chicago Bears as a backup QB, and then in his first 10 starts set an NFL record by going 10-0, breaking the mark formerly set by Steelers QB Mike Kruczek. The mark stood till Ben Roethlisberger broke it in 2004. Tomczak started the in the infamous "Fog Bowl" game for the Bears in the NFC Divisional Playoffs against the Philadelphia Eagles in 1988. In his final regular season start in the NFL was part of the highest-scoring game in Three Rivers Stadium history, losing a shoot-out against the Tennessee Titans 47-36. He threw for 309 yards and two scores in the loss. His NFL career concluded with 73 starts, completing 55.3 percent of his passes for 88 touchdowns and 106 interceptions.
**Nickname:** None
**The Game:** Pittsburgh Steelers vs Kansas City Chiefs in Kansas City, Missouri
October 7, 1996

The Steelers used Tomczak when needed, and in 1994 he led them to a pair of key wins in Week 12 and 13 as the Steelers finished the year 12-4 before falling in a bitterly disappointing AFC Title Game loss to the San Diego Chargers 17-13 at Three Rivers Stadium. In 1995 he again was there when the team called upon him, starting four games after O'Donnell was injured in a Week 1 victory over the Detroit Lions. That season the club made it to the Super Bowl, but couldn't get the job done as the team fell to the Dallas Cowboys 27-17.

That offseason was one of uncertainty for the organization, as their franchise QB in O'Donnell took a mega free agent offer to be the new face of the New York Jets, a deal that even landed him on the cover of *Sports Illustrated*. The QB competition in Pittsburgh turned into a battle between Tomczak, Kordell "Slash" Stewart, and 1994 sixth-round pick Jim Miller.

After a summer battle in Latrobe, PA, at training camp, Cowher went with Miller, a decision that didn't last very long as Tomczak recalls. "That was pretty much the personal highlight for me, 1996. We didn't really have a quarterback that was going to take over the team once Neil [O'Donnell] left and being the elder statesmen and given the opportunity, there was a battle in training camp, and they named Jim Miller the starter for the opener in Jacksonville. By the third quarter I was in there getting most of the snaps, and what ensued over the next fifteen weeks and into the playoffs was quite memorable."

That 1996 season saw Tomczak lead the black and gold to a 10-6 record, and he threw for 2,767 yards and 15 touchdowns, going 10-5 as the team's starter following Week 1. With the help of newly acquired running back Jerome Bettis, the Steelers clinched their fourth AFC Central Title in five seasons, making it to the divisional round of the postseason before falling to the New England Patriots.

# The Game
*By Mike Tomczak*

In 1996, we solidified the quarterback decision a week after I was named the starter. It was Week 2 against Baltimore, and even though we lost our opener at Jacksonville, we got on a pretty good run.

We were able to develop a team identity, all phases were complementary after that first week of the season. We won our next three games after we lost the opener, and then we had a key Monday night game in Kansas City, which was the highlight of the season for me. It put Bill Cowher against his mentor in Marty Schottenheimer, the Chiefs were 4-1, and it was a hostile environment, emotionally charged.

As far as expectations for us, we were in the Super Bowl the year before, so the expectation level was going to be high even with the turnover in our team. That game was really gratifying for me. We ended up going in there and winning that game by 10 points, and I was lucky enough to throw for over 300 yards. I remember multiple times on third down we were able to make conversions to continue drives and keep those guys off the field. They had a guy named Marcus Allen at running back who was pretty potent that we had to account for.

Emotionally the game was charged for me. I had my grandparents and godparents in the audience, they traveled to the game, they lived out that way. The end result was a victory, and I remember [Steelers GM] Tom Donahoe coming up to me after the game and giving me a huge hug and he said, "That was the best performance I've seen in a long, long time for a quarterback." Statistically, I don't know how it ranks or anything, but the bottom line was that it was a hostile environment, and we had numerous third and a bus-ride situations, and we were able to overcome those adversities and complete plays and get first downs. That was a staple game for us, a statement game. It kept us in front in the AFC, not just in the Central division but the AFC as a whole.

We got into the playoffs that year, but we fell short against New England because Jerome Bettis wasn't able to play at 100 percent. It was something from an accountability standpoint, and I was accountable for my play, and my leadership, and it was special being able to bring all these guys together for one cause and be able to win a division championship.

## The Aftermath

Tomczak finished the night in Kansas City going 20-for-32 for 338 yards, helping the Steelers top the Chiefs 17-7. Pittsburgh trailed 7-0 and were down 7-6 until Bettis scored on a 5-yard run in the third quarter in a play that was vintage "Bus," refusing to go down and pushing his way into the end zone to make it 12-7. Tomczak then hit tight end Mark Brunner for a two-point conversion to make it a 14-7 Steelers lead.

The black and gold defense held Chiefs quarterback Steve Bono in check, picking him off twice. They held Allen, who would eventually go on to the Hall of Fame, to just 69 yards on 18 carries. The key stat of the game was the Steelers ability to keep drives alive, as Tomczak mentioned. They went 8-for-14 on third down conversions, while the Chiefs were held to just 5-for-13 in the same stat.

The Steelers' key win in Kansas City was followed by a win over the Cincinnati Bengals at home the following week. After that the team, at 5-1, never seemed to play as well as they had that first six weeks of the year. They went 5-5 the rest of the way, finishing the season with a 10-6 mark, but still good enough to win the AFC Central.

The team hosted the Indianapolis Colts in what was a rematch of their memorable 1995 AFC Title Game from just a year before. With Tomczak under center, the Steelers went into the locker room at halftime down 14-13. Four rushing touchdowns in the second half clinched a dominating 42-13 victory that sent the Steelers to the divisional round the following week against the New England Patriots.

The game in Foxboro was a nightmare, as the Steelers defense, which dominated the Colts by holding them to 146 yards the week before, was shredded for 194 yards on the ground. Curtis Martin ran for 166 yards and three scores in a 28-3 Patriots win that ended Tomczak and the Steelers' season, falling short of another chance at the Super Bowl.

The following season, Tomczak was back on the bench, as Cowher made the move to Stewart as the team's starter at quarterback early in camp. After throwing 401 passes in 1996, Tomczak sat on the sidelines for almost all of 1997, throwing just 24 passes the whole year, 11 of which came in the regular season finale at Tennessee after the Steelers had already wrapped up the year as high as they could go in the AFC.

With Tomczak watching, the Steelers made it to the AFC Title Game before falling to John Elway and the Denver Broncos, 24-21.

Tomczak played two more years with the Steelers, and started the final five games of his career in Pittsburgh, going 1-4 in those games as the team limped to a 6-10 finish in 1999, the worst in the Bill Cowher era. Oddly enough, in his final game as a Steeler, Tomczak went head to head with the quarterback he played behind in 1995 in Pittsburgh. Neil O'Donnell, who was then with the Titans, came on to replace an injured Steve McNair in the 1999 finale.

The two combined to throw for four scores as the Titans outlasted the Steelers 47-36. Tomczak finished his NFL career with the Detroit Lions in 2000, but never appeared in a game or threw a pass. His career concluded with his having thrown for more than 16,000 yards with 87 touchdowns. "It's all memorable. Anytime you have the pleasure of playing in the National Football League, it's all memorable. So you just take it all in."

# CHAPTER 10

# JACK HAM

### Linebacker 1971–1982
### December 29, 1974 vs Oakland Raiders at Oakland Coliseum
### PITTSBURGH STEELERS 24 - OAKLAND RAIDERS 13

When you think about great linebackers in Pittsburgh Steelers history, the name Jack Ham has to be right at the top of the list.

Ham was elected to the Pro Football Hall of Fame in 1988, and it is not unusual to see him on the lists of various publications as one of the "Top 100 Football Players of All Time."

The native of Johnstown, Pennsylvania, was a standout linebacker at Penn State, where for three years he was a starter. He was an All-American his senior season, recording four interceptions and amassing 91 tackles.

He joined the Steelers in 1971, and made an impact at the linebacker spot right away. He started 13 games his rookie season, and in his second season collected seven interceptions as the team marched to an 11-3 record and into the playoffs.

It was that 1972 season that the Steelers' epic rivalry with the Oakland Raiders really kicked into high gear. It was on December 23 1972, when a late miracle touchdown by Franco Harris called the "Immaculate Reception" pushed the Steelers to a 13-7 win in the Divisional Playoffs.

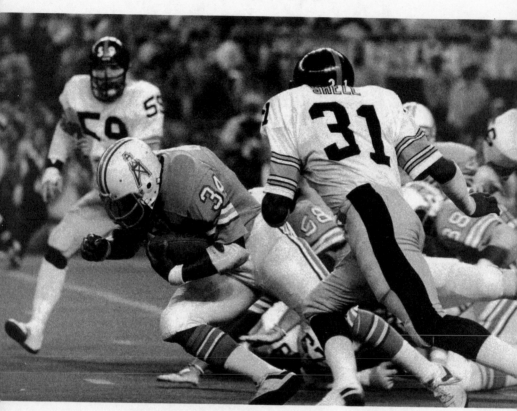

**Jack Ham (l) and Donnie Shell converge on Earl Campbell.**

*AP Photo/Ed Kolenovsky*

## Notes on Jack Ham

| | |
|---|---|
| **Years Played:** | 1971–1982 |
| **Position:** | Linebacker |
| **Height:** | 6'2" |
| **Weight:** | 225 |
| **Hometown:** | Johnstown, Pennsylvania |
| **Current Residence:** | Sewickley Heights, Pennsylvania |
| **Occupation:** | Sports Analyst for Penn State Radio Network |
| **Accomplishments:** | Played his entire football career in Pennsylvania from high school (Johnstown), college (Penn State), and twelve seasons with the Steelers, winning four Super Bowls. Was the Steelers second-round pick, 34th overall, in 1971. Was All-Pro for six seasons and was named to eight straight Pro Bowls, ending his career with 37 interceptions, including 32 during the regular season, third highest in NFL history among linebackers when he walked away from the game in 1983. Was the only unanimous defensive choice on the NFL's Team of the Decade for the 1970s. Career statistics include 25 sacks, 21 fumbles recovered. His 53 takeaways are the most in NFL history by a non-defensive back. Was inducted into the Pro Football Hall of Fame in 1988. In 2014 Ham was named by the Big Ten Network as part of "The Mount Rushmore of Penn State Football." |
| **Nickname:** | "Dobre Shunka" (Polish for "good ham") |
| **The Game:** | Pittsburgh Steelers vs Oakland Raiders in Oakland, California<br>December 29, 1974 |

The Steelers-Raiders rivalry was the fiercest in the NFL in the 1970s. They were two teams in the same conference that simply didn't like each other.

From 1972 to 1976 the Steelers and Raiders met five straight seasons in the playoffs, and in three of those games it was for the right to represent the AFC in the Super Bowl.

Ham was in the middle of a lot of those battles with the Raiders, including the AFC Title Game in 1974, a game that more than one Steelers Hall of Famer has called the most important game in the history of the entire Steelers organization.

# The Game
*By Jack Ham*

The most important and favorite game of my career had to be the AFC Championship Game against the Raiders before we went to our first Super Bowl, played in Oakland in December of 1974.

We were playing on the road, number one, and I am sure if Oakland and Pittsburgh had been in different conferences we might have met up in quite a few Super Bowls.

We had battles with those guys throughout the course of my career, and when you go through the whole thing, either Pittsburgh or the Raiders were always involved in the championship games or in the Super Bowls.

Oakland had beaten Miami the week before, and people thought that was such a great game and that the Raiders would waltz into the Super Bowl.

They were a great football team, there was no question about that. Our front four kind of dominated them against the run, and we made enough big plays in that game to catapult us into the Super Bowl.

I don't enjoy flying all that much, but that five-hour plane ride afterward, I was sitting in the back of the plane with Joe Greene.

When you're going to your first Super Bowl, and you have won a game to put you in that Super Bowl, it is very, very special. That is by far the most fun I had, including Super Bowls, playing in a football game.

That game not only catapulted our football team to our first Super Bowl, but kind of got us on the right track.

We were a good football team prior to that year, then we went and drafted Lynn Swann, John Stallworth, Jack Lambert, and Mike Webster. They were all rookies that year, but we really ended up being a great football team with that draft.

The Raiders' win over Miami the week before was such a marquee game. Miami had already had their undefeated season and they had great years and won some championships, and then we beat the Raiders, which was also a great football team.

This Raiders football team, like I said, if it wasn't us, it was the Raiders. To win it on the road—well, normally you don't win conference championships on the road.

That win was closer than most people feel. The Raiders ran the ball for just 29 yards; to win the game like that was truly special.

I had two interceptions in the game, and the second one was key because of when it happened. We had a safety blitz called on the play, and to be candid it wasn't really a hard play to make.

I was drifting out and they were trying to throw the ball to the running back, he was the check down on the play. We had the blitz coming at [Raiders' QB Ken] Stabler, and he tried to throw the ball outside in the flat.

I saw their running back, Charlie Smith, and I saw Stabler throwing it and I peeled off the running back and cut underneath him on the sideline and made the play.

With the blitz coming, with Jack Lambert and Glen Edwards coming up the middle, Stabler had to get rid of the football.

I love Kenny [Stabler], but that was not one of his better passes. I don't know if he didn't see me out there or what but that's a play and a throw you really don't want to make.

We had played the Raiders enough the past couple of years, we had the "Immaculate Reception" here in Pittsburgh and we played them in the playoffs the following year, and I think we both knew just how good a football team the other was.

They knew how good they were, they knew how good we were. That day our front four just did a better job. The Raiders were such a greatly balanced team. You can talk about Kenny Stabler, but they ran the ball effectively, there was really great balance to their offense.

They ran most of their plays to the left, with Art Shell, Gene Upshaw, and Dave Casper. From my side of it that's why I was in the passing game a lot, it wasn't so much physical for me because I was on the open end side.

Normally teams are right-handed for the most part when running the ball. But not the Raiders. So I was involved in the passing game a lot, which I loved doing anyway.

Maybe that's another reason why I loved this game so much. It was usually a physical game against the Raiders, but not so much for me. I was almost like another safety playing back there for the most part.

The Raiders could beat you in so many different ways; you love challenges like that when you're playing against a team like that. Their offensive line was just fabulous.

Sadly, he's no longer with us, but Ernie Holmes had one of the best games I've ever seen anyone play, and he would line up every play on Gene Upshaw. He just dominated play along with Joe Greene and the rest of that front four.

Everybody was making big plays. I remember Lambert making a play on a pass throw to Cliff Branch, he was the only guy in the middle of the field. It was a two-deep zone, and Lambert drifted really deep and there was no one there in the open field and he brought down Cliff Branch.

So many big plays in that game. We all knew that you didn't have to get up for the Raiders, you didn't need any speech from Chuck Noll to get ready to play in Oakland; it was a given.

## The Aftermath

The win over the Raiders in the AFC Championship Game in 1974 sparked the Steelers to their first Super Bowl win two weeks later, as they beat the Minnesota Vikings 16-6 in New Orleans.

Ham was part of a Steelers defense that many say was the greatest in NFL history. With the front four of the "Steel Curtain," along with fellow Hall of Fame linebacker Jack Lambert, and a great secondary that featured another Hall of Famer in Mel Blount, the Steelers were hard to beat.

The team won four championships in six seasons, their final one of the era coming in 1979 when they beat the Los Angeles Rams 31-19.

Ham amassed an incredible career with the Steelers over the twelve years with the franchise. He was named to eight Pro Bowls, was named six times to the first All-Pro team, and holds the NFL Record for most career forced turnovers by a linebacker with 53.

Ham's speed, along with his ability to create turnovers, made him one of the most dangerous linebackers in the game in the 1970s.

It wasn't a shock that he was named to the Pittsburgh Steelers All-Time Team, and his jersey number 59 is no longer issued by the franchise.

Upon retirement in 1982, Ham moved to the broadcast booth, doing work as a color man for NFL games on the radio, and even at one point co-hosting a show during the NFL season.

Ham was even a minority owner of the Johnstown Tomahawks, a team in the North American Hockey League.

At sixty-six years old, Ham remains active in business and is still beloved as one of the greatest Steelers of all time.

It's hard even to this day to find a better big-play linebacker than the one that wore #59 for twelve years during the greatest era of Steelers football.

# CHAPTER 11

# JEROME BETTIS

## Running Back 1996–2005

### December 11, 2005 vs Chicago Bears at Heinz Field

### PITTSBURGH STEELERS 21 - CHICAGO BEARS 9

He is one of the most popular players in the history of the Pittsburgh Steelers organization. A running back that was basically given away to the Steelers on draft day in 1996, and went on to have a Hall of Fame career that saw him step away from the spotlight of the game just moments after becoming a champion on the platform in Detroit, Michigan, after being on the winning side of Super Bowl XL.

For Jerome Bettis, it truly was a storybook career in the Steel City.

No one could have imagined when the Steelers made a draft-day deal with the Los Angeles Rams on April 20, 1996, along with a third-round pick for a second-round selection in the same draft and a fourth-round selection in the 1997 draft, that Bettis would go on to be the best "big man" running back the NFL had seen since Hall of Famer Earl Campbell of the Houston Oilers.

He ran over defenders, helping the Steelers reach the postseason six times, the AFC Title Game three times, and finally obtaining a win in Super Bowl XL in 2005. His best season with the Steelers came in 2000 when he ran for 1,341 yards and eight touchdowns.

He was moved into the background more than once during his Steelers career, but was always there when called upon. He saved the team in

AP Photo/Keith Srakocic

# Notes on Jerome Bettis

| | |
|---|---|
| **Years Played:** | 1996–2005 |
| **Position:** | Running Back |
| **Height:** | 5'11" |
| **Weight:** | 251 |
| **Hometown:** | Detroit, Michigan |
| **Current Residence:** | Roswell, Georgia |
| **Occupation:** | NFL Analyst for ESPN |
| **Accomplishments:** | Drafted 10th overall by the Los Angeles Rams in 1993. Joined the Steelers via trade on draft day 1996. A six-time Pro Bowler and two-time All-Pro. Took over as the Steelers feature back in 1996, and in first two seasons ran for over 3,000 yards on the ground and 18 touchdowns. His best season on the ground came in 1997 when he ran for 1665 yards and seven touchdowns. Late Steelers Radio color commentator Myron Cope started Bettis' nickname "The Bus" after hearing a brother of a fellow Notre Dame alumni call Jerome "Bussy." Bettis finished his 13 NFL seasons as the NFL's fifth all-time leading rusher with 13,662 yards and 91 touchdowns. He also caught 200 passes for 1,449 yards and three touchdowns. Retired on the platform after the Steelers won Super Bowl XL 21-10 over the Seattle Seahawks. Went into the Pro Football Hall of Fame in August of 2015. |
| **Nickname:** | "The Bus" |
| **The Game:** | Pittsburgh Steelers vs Chicago Bears in Pittsburgh, Pennsylvania December 11, 2005 |

1994 when high-profile free agent pickup Deuce Staley went down with an injury.

In 2005 he stepped up again, helping out new starter Willie Parker and making sure that when the game was on the line and the team needed that extra yard, he would be there. Bettis' enthusiasm and energy, along with his blue-collar work ethic, made him a fan favorite from day one with Steeler Nation.

Broadcaster Myron Cope took Bettis' college nickname "The Bus" from the University of Notre Dame and introduced it to Steeler fans worldwide. It was commonplace to see cardboard buses at Steeler games, and announcers on both TV and radio commonly referred to Bettis as "The Bus" for a good part of his Steelers career.

Bettis will go down as one of the great backs in Steelers history along with the likes of Franco Harris and John Henry Johnson, and is immortalized with the highest honor a player can get: a bust in Canton, Ohio, at the Pro Football Hall of Fame.

# The Game

*By Jerome Bettis*

I think of a lot of games, but I think the one game that's remembered the most is the Chicago game in my final season. It's the one that people draw the correlation between me and the game, or the one picture, and it's playing against Chicago.

It was snowing, it was muddy out there, and it was a critical game, because the Chicago Bears had the best defense in the NFL. We were at the time 7-5, so we had to win the last four games just to get in the playoffs.

So we had no choice, we had to win out. We had just lost the week before to Cincinnati at home, and so the first game, the next game, was this huge game against the best defense in the NFL. So we couldn't afford to lose another game, and we had the best defense in the league coming into town. This was not good. That was the mindset going into that week.

I'll never forget coach Cowher the week of the game. We used to have this big chart, and on it was all sixteen weeks of the season. So he walked in our first meeting of the week, and all the weeks are erased and all it said on the board was "Chicago Bears."

He told us, forget about the past, it's one game, it's a one-game season. Then he said, "I want everyone to grade themselves in the Cincinnati game, I want every guy to write down plus or minus for every play that you were in." So we went into that game, and the field was a mess. It was slick, it was slippery, and early on [running back] Willie Parker couldn't get going, he couldn't get his footing and kept slipping.

I only had one carry for one yard in the first half, but we went in at halftime and had the lead, and the field kept getting worse with the snow falling.

Then in the second half, they went to me sixteen times, and I was able to rush for over 100 yards in the second half of that football game, and it really propelled us to winning a championship. So that game was huge in our championship run because that game in essence became our first playoff game.

By the time we got to the playoffs we had played four playoff games When everyone else was getting ready for the playoffs, we were in the middle of our playoff run.

## The Aftermath

The 21-9 win over the Bears was the last 100-yard rushing game of Jerome Bettis' career, but it could not have come at a more critical time.

"The Bus" wound up the afternoon rushing for 101 yards on 17 carries, a 5.9-yards-per-carry average and two touchdowns.

Many Steelers fans will always recall the touchdown that sealed the win about five minutes into the third quarter. The play was a simple off-tackle run in which Bettis, from the Bears' five-yard line, was met by Chicago superstar linebacker Brian Urlacher.

The 255-pound Bettis bowled over Urlacher as the last line of Chicago defense, pushing his way into the end zone and, at the time, a 21-3 Steelers lead.

The Hall of Fame back was unaware of how iconic that moment would become when it happened, a play that Steelers voice Bill Hillgrove described as the play that defined Bettis as a running back.

"When you are playing the game you don't realize and you are not able to capture that moment, and that moment became so big, but it was just an instant in the game, and I'm just fighting trying to get a touchdown for our team to get us a win.

"Time doesn't stand still for that moment, you don't necessarily realize how significant that moment is for your career. Later on, the play started, and more so the picture, because they were able to capture that moment and freeze it in time."

The win over the Bears started a winning streak that by the time it was done saw the Steelers win eight in a row—four games in the regular season to earn the sixth seed in the AFC, and then four in the playoffs to take home their fifth world championship, and send Bettis into retirement a champion for the first time in his career.

Bettis' final home game with the Steelers took place in Week 17, and it was a must-win for the team to get into the postseason against his hometown team, the Detroit Lions. The back scored three touchdowns that day, as the Steelers rolled to a 35-21 win to earn the last playoff spot in the AFC.

"It was very appropriate that the final home game was the Detroit Lions, so everybody back in Detroit got an opportunity to see me play my last game in Heinz Field."

The playoff run almost saw Bettis end his career on one of the more sour notes any player would have to endure. In the AFC Divisional Game against the heavily favored Indianapolis Colts, the Steelers led 21-18 with 1:20 left, the Steelers defense having just stopped the Colts at their own two-yard line.

Bettis was called upon to shut the door, as Cowher gave him the ball to score what should have been an easy touchdown to seal the win. Instead, Bettis fumbled the ball, and the Colts recovered and took the ball to their own 42-yard line with plenty of time left.

Colts QB Peyton Manning got Indianapolis in position for a game-tying field goal attempt that would have sent the game into overtime, but kicker Mike Vanderjagt pushed the ball wide, saving Bettis and the Steelers sending the sixth seed to the AFC Championship Game in Denver.

After a dominating win in the AFC Title Game in Denver the following week, the Steelers beat the Seattle Seahawks 21-10 to win Super Bowl XL, a game in which Bettis ran for 43 yards on 14 carries, grinding out some tough yards late to keep the clock moving with the Steelers ahead.

Bettis ended his career with 13,662 yards and 91 touchdowns. While it took a few years, he finally got the call the night before Super Bowl XLIX in 2015 that he was going into the Pro Football Hall of Fame. "Once you get in it gives you an opportunity to reflect back, because now my career is completely done, there are no more levels to attain.

"This is it, and now I have the opportunity to stand among the greatest players to have ever played the game. That's the amazing part. It's something that, because I was so busy trying to get in, I couldn't really appreciate."

Bettis is still heavily involved with a pair of foundations, the Jerome Bettis Bus Stops Here Foundation and the Jerome Bettis Asthma and Sports Camp, which he is a part of annually to assist children with asthma. Bettis himself had been diagnosed with asthma at the age of fourteen.

# CHAPTER 12

# TYRONE CARTER

### Safety 2004–2009

**February 1, 2009 vs Arizona Cardinals at Raymond James Stadium**

**PITTSBURGH STEELERS 27 - ARIZONA CARDINALS 23**

The Pittsburgh Steelers of 2008 had a type of "legendary" look to them, a team that ranked first in the NFL and played one of the toughest schedules, if not the toughest, that season in the NFL.

The defense boasted two of the best defensive players in the game in outside linebacker James Harrison, the 2008 NFL Defensive Player of the Year, and safety Troy Polamalu who was game changer in the secondary.

There were many complementary players on that defense, one of which was a solid backup safety named Tyrone Carter.

Carter joined the Steelers in 2004 as a free agent, and after three seasons with the New York Jets and one with the Minnesota Vikings he realized right away the difference playing in the Steel City.

"When I got to the Steelers in 2004 I really got a different perspective of team concept," Carter said. "Not only team but organization from the top down. Everybody believed in the same goals and worked towards those same goals."

AP Photo/Rob Carr

## Notes on Tyrone Carter

**Years Played:** 2004–2009

**Position:** Safety

**Height:** 5'9"

**Weight:** 195

**Hometown:** Fort Lauderdale, Florida

**Current Residence:** Minneapolis, Minnesota

**Occupation:** Owner of TC Elite Training School (Football Camps)

**Accomplishments:** Carter was named by the Miami Sun-Sentinel as an all-county defensive first-team choice as a senior. He also received Miami Herald all-county offensive first team honors as a running back, putting up 1,349 yards and 23 touchdowns as a senior. Earned All-American honors and won several national awards while playing in college at the University of Minnesota. Drafted in the fourth round by the Minnesota Vikings in 2000. Joined the Steelers as a free agent in October of 2004. Part of two Steelers Super Bowl winning teams in 2005 (XL) and 2008 (XLIII) and was a two-time AFC Defensive Player of the Week winner with the Steelers. Carter's career wrapped up with nine interceptions and two touchdowns over an 11-season NFL career that ended with stints in Washington and San Diego.

**Nickname:** None

**The Game:** Pittsburgh Steelers vs Arizona Cardinals in Tampa, Florida
February 1, 2009

The safety was a solid addition to the roster, collecting three interceptions in that 2008 season, and taking home an AFC Defensive Player of the Week award during a Week 17 victory against the Cleveland Browns as a warmup for the team's Super Bowl run.

Carter already had a Super Bowl ring on his resume as he was with the team in 2005 when they beat the Seattle Seahawks for their fifth title, and in 2008 the Fort Lauderdale, Florida, native felt the team was even closer off the field.

"We were a close team, and being a close team will carry you farther than anything … because you eat, breathe, sleep, and do everything together," Carter said.

"Having that common area showed me a whole different mindset about the game and taught me the game as well."

The safety played in all three postseason games, including an interception during the team's 23-14 victory over the Baltimore Ravens in the AFC Championship Game to advance to Super Bowl XLIII, a game that still ranks as one of the best Super Bowls in history.

# The Game
*By Tyrone Carter*

For me, I feel like I had a lot of good games that I remember, and that will always stick with me, but the most important ones were the Super Bowls, especially Super Bowl XLIII when we took on the Arizona Cardinals.

That game we found ourselves down, we had to make stops, and James Harrison picked off a ball and took it 100 yards for a touchdown.

Then we were trailing with less than a minute left and Santonio Holmes scored the winning touchdown, making a toe-tapping catch in the back corner of the end zone.

We always played for sixty minutes, as long as there was still time on that clock we felt we had opportunities and put ourselves in position to win games.

With that in mind we never doubted ourselves, we just knew we would fight to the end, and that's the type of team we had. We never gave up, we never quit, never wavered. We always stood up for each other.

Knowing that we had time left, we had full confidence in ourselves that our offense would come away and make a winning drive.

The last series after we scored the touchdown and the Cardinals had the ball with under a minute left, I recall I played on that series because they kept changing formations.

At the time I was coming in on the corner packages, and we knew they had to pass the ball to get the ball downfield.

With Kurt Warner as their quarterback, we knew he couldn't move in the pocket with our pass rushers LaMarr Woodley and James Harrison on the outside.

We just had to hold our end on the back end in the secondary so they didn't get any big throws like they had earlier with Larry Fitzgerald.

That game will always stick in my mind, and will always stick with me.

The Steelers organization was a great organization to play with. It was a team, family oriented: the organization that I love.

The defense that season in 2008, we had a swag to us. We just felt like if we continued to give our offense the ball, and we continued to play our "A" game, we had a chance to win every game.

I just think that being around that defense, that Steeler defense, it was the focal point of the organization, and we knew that we won championships defensively.

Our players and teammates—James Farrior, James Harrison—we had a lot of guys that shared the whole wealth of making sure each guy was accountable.

We went into every game feeling like we could stop our opponent from getting any points or big plays, and like we had a chance to win every game.

It was a mindset back then that defense was going to win us games, and defense was going to keep us in games.

We had an offense with Ben Roethlisberger, always looking to throw downfield and make plays for us, and all we needed to do was continue to get them that ball.

It was awesome to be a part of that, and to be able to come away with two Super Bowl wins, and not just the wins but the journeys to get us there.

I remember when I got to Pittsburgh in 2004 we lost to New England in the AFC Championship Game, and that week Hines [Ward] cried, Ben [Roethlisberger] cried, and we told each other that we would never have that taste again.

We looked forward to the next year and it was awesome to be able to get right back there the next year and win the Super Bowl when we beat the Seahawks.

It showed the character of our team. The method we put into that, it was all about family, and that's why I always say the Steelers organization is the best in the NFL.

When I look back, that was a great game. It simplifies that message we always said, that situational football exists in the game, and during the game you have to be able to weather the storm sometimes and continue to stay focused on the task at hand. That's how you come away with the victory.

That's what we were able to do. It was a veteran team, veteran leadership. Guys didn't let each other get down on each other when the going got tough, we continued to lift each other up, continued to believe.

That game showed the true character and the true commitment of that team as far as us being able to get the job done and coming away with the victory.

## The Aftermath

Carter was a piece of the puzzle for two championship teams with the Steelers, a player who was never mentioned in the headlines, but was always there when needed.

He played one more season for the Steelers in 2009, and that season had a memorable game in Week 9 in Denver.

Carter got the start for Ryan Clark, and upon stepping in, returned an interception 48 yards for a touchdown, and collected a second pick to seal the win with less than two minutes left.

For his efforts, Carter was the AFC Defensive Player of the Week. He played a big part in that season, starting four games at the start of the year, and then eight for an injured Troy Polamalu to finish the season.

At age thirty-one, Carter played one more season, signing with the San Diego Chargers and appearing in seven games.

His career ended appearing in a total of 158 games with nine picks and two touchdowns. In six years with the Steelers, Carter played in 89 games with 4.5 sacks and six interceptions.

He still looks back on his time with the Steelers as the best of his life, drawing upon nothing but fond memories, including a number of special ones that 2008 season as the franchise collected its NFL record sixth Super Bowl title.

"I'm so blessed to be able to have that opportunity to play for the Steelers for six years and come away with two Super Bowl rings," Carter said.

"We had great coaches, as well as a great owner. I am a Steeler till I die."

CHAPTER **13**

# JASON GILDON

### Outside Linebacker 1994–2003

**January 27, 2002 vs New England Patriots at Heinz Field**

**NEW ENGLAND PATRIOTS 24 - PITTSBURGH STEELERS 17**

When you talk about the linebacker position and the Pittsburgh Steelers, there are always certain names that just seem to roll off your tongue.

From Hall of Famers like Jack Lambert and Jack Ham, to Mike Merriweather in the 1980s, then to the 1990s with the outside combo of Greg Lloyd and Kevin Greene, to even more current stars like James Harrison, the linebacker spot in the Steel City has always been held up to a certain level.

One player that deserves to be talked about among the great linebackers in Steelers history is the man who holds the team's sack record, Jason Gildon.

Drafted in the fourth round in the 1994 draft from Oklahoma State, Gildon stepped right in and in his first two years was a force on the Steelers special teams unit.

In 1996 he got his first shot at making an impact on the outside, as Lloyd went down for the season in the regular season opener at Jacksonville, and eventually Gildon found himself being called upon.

By the time Gildon got his shot he was ready, as he had been an understudy of Lloyd and Greene for a couple of seasons, when the

99

AP Photo/ Roberto Borea

# Notes on Jason Gildon

| | |
|---|---|
| **Years Played:** | 1994–2003 |
| **Position:** | Linebacker |
| **Height:** | 6'4" |
| **Weight:** | 255 |
| **Hometown:** | Altus, Oklahoma |
| **Current Residence:** | Pittsburgh, Pennsylvania |
| **Occupation:** | High School Football Coach at Cardinal Wuerl North High School in Cranberry Township, PA |
| **Accomplishments:** | Was the Steelers third-round pick, 88th overall, in the 1994 NFL Draft out of the University of Oklahoma State. Played special teams in the first two seasons then took over for Greg Lloyd in 1996 and recorded seven sacks his first season, and never left the position. The current Steelers All-Time Sack Leader with 80 sacks, breaking the mark of L.C. Greenwood. Sacked Arizona Cardinals QB Jeff Blake for the record in Week 9 of the 2003 season. Ended his career with 520 tackles, 44 passes defensed, two interceptions, and three defensive touchdowns. Made the Pro Bowl in 2000, 2001, and 2002, and was All-Pro in 2001. Best season in 2000 put up 13.5 sacks, 75 tackles, and one defensive touchdown. Finished his NFL career with the Jacksonville Jaguars in 2004 after going to training camp with the Buffalo Bills. |
| **Nickname:** | None |
| **The Game:** | Pittsburgh Steelers vs New England Patriots in Pittsburgh, Pennsylvania January 27, 2002 |

Steelers played in the 1994 AFC Title Game and in 1995 when they played in Super Bowl XXX.

"My first year there I came into a system and I came in behind two already established outside linebackers, already All-Pro outside linebackers," Gildon said.

"A guy right out of college not really knowing what to expect and these were great guys, took me under their wing, they showed me what it meant to be a professional."

Gildon followed in the strong tradition of great Steelers linebackers, as he amassed 54 sacks in five seasons dating from 1998 to 2002.

By the time his final season with the Steelers took place in 2003, he was upon the cusp of breaking the team's all-time sack record held by L.C. Greenwood.

In a November game at Heinz Field against the Arizona Cardinals in the midst of a tough 6-10 season, Gildon broke Greenwood's sack record with a takedown of Jeff Blake in the third quarter to set the new mark that stands to this day.

Playing linebacker was special to Gildon, something he remembers fondly and cherishes as he now coaches young men at Cardinal Wuerl North Catholic in Cranberry, Pennsylvania.

"I can remember just having that sense of urgency playing that position," Gildon said of playing linebacker for the Steelers.

"To be a Pittsburgh Steeler linebacker it adds a little more to it, it puts you in sort of a rarefied air, I think the guys that have been able to play it and be successful realize it."

# The Game
*By Jason Gildon*

Unfortunately, the game that I can remember the most is the game that we lost in the 2001 season, the AFC Championship Game at home to the Patriots.

It was a great game against a quality opponent, despite the fact that we were down early, we kind of had to stay the course there.

We gave up two touchdowns that day on special teams, so defensively we really had to dig in. I think it showed a lot about our character defensively, to really just stem the tide.

They capitalized, especially on the special teams aspect of it. At that point, you go into every game with a game plan, but no one plans on being 14 or 21 points down.

I think at that point things changed, and we really just couldn't get back on track. They only scored three points after they led 21-3.

Everyone thought it was over, but I was proud of the fact that we continually went out and put up stops. We gave our team a chance to win, despite the odds.

We had some chances on defense to put some points on the board, it was basically a tale of two halves. They had to finish the game with Drew Bledsoe at quarterback, it was one of those games in my mind where we could have pulled it out.

I know Joey Porter almost had an interception, and I almost had one early in the second half, a ball that I batted down and I should have caught. The game really had a lot of ups and downs in it.

That whole day, that whole game, you couldn't ask for anything more as a football player, I think. You come out to a game, and you really don't know what to expect, and then all of a sudden you look up and you are down big.

At that moment, one of two things can happen: you can stem the tide and keep doing what you've been doing, or you can choose to give up, and concede the outcome.

Looking back, I don't think we were overconfident, I think that it was a big game, and sometimes when it's a big game, things don't turn out like you planned. I think I learned a lot about myself and I think I learned a lot about the guys that played in that game with me on the defensive side. There was no quit in us, and we took the field every series like "this is going to be the one that turns it around for us."

We lost sight of some of the little things that we did well, that we took for granted, and the Patriots were able to capitalize on it.

It was kind of the ushering in of the Patriots era, the early part of the 2000s. It's interesting, you look at Tom Brady now, and there he is out there still doing it and doing it at a high level. Just seeing how he's been able to keep up with the times, and the change of the position.

In my mind though, I feel we could have pulled it out, we should have pulled it out, but unfortunately we didn't.

## The Aftermath

The home AFC Title Game loss to the Patriots was one of a long line of stinging home title game losses in the Bill Cowher era.

It wouldn't be the last time New England beat the Steelers in a title game in Pittsburgh, as in 2004 they repeated the feat, beating the Steelers in Ben Roethlisberger's rookie season, 41-27.

The loss in 2001 was defined by two huge special teams miscues by the Steelers that opened the door for New England to build a 21-3 lead midway through the third quarter.

The first was a penalty on wide out Troy Edwards allowing New England to gain a few yards, and more importantly, another chance at a punt return in the first quarter.

The penalty paved the way for Troy Brown to return a Josh Miller punt 55 yards to give New England a 7-0 lead.

The second huge special teams mistake came in the third quarter. Already down 14-3, the Steelers started the third quarter driving to the Patriots 16, but were forced to settle for a Kris Brown 34-yard field goal attempt.

New England's Brandon Mitchell blocked the kick, and Antwan Harris wound up with the ball in the end zone moments later to make it a 21-3 game, and many in Heinz Field felt the game was basically over.

The Steelers didn't quit, as they fought back with touchdowns from Jerome Bettis and Amos Zereoue. Each scored to close it to 21-17 late in the quarter.

The fourth quarter saw the Steelers run out of magic. Quarterback Kordell Stewart threw two huge interceptions, one to Tebucky Jones and another to Lawyer Milloy, ending the Steelers' dreams of playing the St. Louis Rams in Super Bowl XXXVI with a 24-17 setback.

Gildon played two more seasons with the Steelers, as the team reached the postseason in 2002 before losing to the Tennessee Titans in the divisional round.

In 2003 the team slipped to 6-10, their worst season under Bill Cowher. Gildon put up six sacks, good enough to pass Greenwood for the team's all-time mark for sacks.

Gildon ended his Steelers career with 77 sacks, leaving the team following the 2003 campaign. He finished his career in Jacksonville with the Jaguars in 2004 before retiring.

Gildon now uses his football knowledge to help mold young men on the football field as the head coach of Cardinal Wuerl North Catholic. He takes the same approach with his high school kids that he learned in his ten seasons with the Steelers.

"The Pittsburgh Steelers, in my opinion, is one of, if not the best organizations in the NFL," Gildon said.

"I think the way they approach winning, the way they handle players, the way they choose their coaches is definitely top notch."

# CHAPTER 14

# CHAD BROWN

### Linebacker 1993–1996
### October 13, 1996 vs Cincinnati Bengals at Three Rivers Stadium
### PITTSBURGH STEELERS 20 - CINCINNATI BENGALS 10

Injuries can open a door for a good player to become a star, and in the case of former Steelers linebacker Chad Brown, that very thing happened in the 1996 season.

Brown was a second-round draft pick for the Steelers in 1993 out of the University of Colorado, and worked his way into being a starter for the Steelers in just his second season.

To this day he recalls with great fondness the beginning of his career, one that saw him introduced to the Steelers organization getting an early taste of the legacy of the franchise.

"Playing for the Pittsburgh Steelers is essentially like playing for football royalty," Brown recalls. "When you're drafted to the Steelers, that first rookie mini-camp, they took the rookies to the team hotel, and they showed them highlights of Steeler greatness, and the video ended with Hall of Fame speeches from former Steelers.

"As a young rookie that was so impactful for me, and once the video ended some of those guys walked into the room, and you got a chance to meet those guys. It really set the tone for what you're about to get into. It was awesome, just incredible.

"It was really profound and very deep, and gave me an instant appreciation of what I was joining up on to."

Brown was very good as an inside linebacker, and in 1994 on a defense that was simply dominating, he played and started in all sixteen games, and put up 90 tackles, 8.5 sacks, and an interception.

The team went 12-4 and made it to the AFC Championship Game before falling in a bitter home loss to the San Diego Chargers, 17-13.

The following year Brown struggled with injuries, appearing and starting in just ten of the team's games during the regular season.

He was on the field and started all three of the team's postseason games, starting at inside linebacker in Super Bowl XXX as the black and gold fell to the Dallas Cowboys 27-17.

The following summer Brown could not have guessed what was coming for him as he entered his final year under contract with the Steelers.

That offseason the team was in transition despite being the defending AFC Champions.

They lost starting quarterback Neil O'Donnell via free agency to the New York Jets, but felt their defense, with a returning healthy cornerback Rod Woodson, who missed most of 1995 after tearing his ACL, would once again make them contenders.

Little did they know that on opening day 1996 in Jacksonville, disaster would strike in the form of another huge season-ending injury to a star on their defense.

That hot afternoon Pro Bowl outside linebacker Greg Lloyd tore the patella tendon in his left knee, and would be forced to miss the rest of the season.

The injury also opened the door for Brown, who moved from the inside to the outside, and became another star linebacker for the Steelers.

"Jacksonville beat us that opening game. It was incredibly hot, and I remember their coach, Tom Coughlin, did the smart thing, and they wore their white jerseys at home," Brown said.

"I remember Levon and I talking in the huddle, and I literally felt like my brain was melting. We were wearing those black jerseys, and it felt like we were melting away.

"They had a good game plan for us, kept us on the field most of the game. Guys were getting injured; it was a rough start to that year, and we had to go through a transition.

*Photo courtesy of Chad Brown*

## Notes on Chad Brown

| | |
|---|---|
| **Years Played:** | 1993–1996 |
| **Position:** | Linebacker |
| **Height:** | 6'2" |
| **Weight:** | 245 |
| **Hometown:** | Altadena, California |
| **Current Residence:** | Littleton, Colorado |
| **Occupation:** | Sells non-venomous snakes through a business he owns called Pro Exotics |
| **Accomplishments:** | Was a four-year starter at Colorado. Drafted in the second-round, 44th overall, of the 1993 NFL Draft by the Steelers. Was awarded the "1993 Joe Greene Great Performance Award" with the Steelers. Played on the inside at the linebacker spot for the Steelers until an injury to Greg Lloyd in 1996 moved him to the outside, where he had a career year with 13 sacks and two interceptions. Ended his NFL career with 1,088 tackles, 79 sacks, and six interceptions in 188 career games. Was a three-time Pro Bowler (1996, 1998, 1999) and two-time All-Pro (1996, 1998). Signed with the Seattle Seahawks following the 1996 season, playing eight seasons in Seattle and was named to the Seattle Seahawks 35th Anniversary Team. |
| **Nickname:** | None |
| **The Game:** | Pittsburgh Steelers vs Cincinnati Bengals in Pittsburgh, Pennsylvania<br>October 13, 1996 |

"When you miss your defensive heartbeat in Greg Lloyd, the guy that sets the tone every practice, every game, every meeting, not only does he set it with his intensity, but his incredibly physical style of play, there's going to be an adjustment on the team to see who is going to emerge."

The player that emerged was Brown, who had a breakout season in 1996, recording 13 sacks, two interceptions, three forced fumbles, and two recoveries.

It was a memorable season for Brown, who, despite leaving the team following that season, made the most of his chance to, for one season, move to outside linebacker and be an even bigger part of a dominating Steelers defense.

# The Game

*By Chad Brown*

There are so many games, but one of the games that comes to mind is a breakout game I had against Cincinnati in 1996.

Greg [Lloyd] was injured the first game against Jacksonville, and Bill Cowher asked me to move outside, and those first couple of games were a transition.

It was not only a transition for me in terms of positions, but on our defense as a whole because we no longer had Greg Lloyd, and we didn't have that leadership there anymore.

It was kind of a growing up phase for Levon [Kirkland] and I to take on a little more leadership, but also for me to try and fill the impossible void that Greg Lloyd left, not being on the field every week.

That Cincinnati game, it was the first game my daughter ever came to, so it was special in that perspective. She was born in August of that offseason, so she was just about three months old when we played the Bengals.

It was a great game for me. I had four and a half sacks, an interception, caused a fumble, and had 10 tackles.

That game was when I kind of got rid of all the timidity and uncertainty about playing Greg's position, and I was really able to go out and play the position the way I wanted to play it.

There was an aspect early on of trying to go out there and replace the guy that I regarded as the absolute baddest man in football, and in a way being able to fill his shoes. There was also a team aspect to it and a personal aspect, as well. I always thought I could play well at that position.

I always wanted to prove myself because I did so as an inside linebacker and an outside linebacker in college, and that was the first step to me proving myself as an outside linebacker in the National Football League.

Eric Bieniemy was the third down back for the Bengals that game, and he was my college teammate at the University of Colorado.

There's rivalry and competition that comes with going against a former college teammate, and Eric, while a good player, was just not big enough to block me.

Dick LeBeau, our defensive coordinator, had come up with some schemes that put me one-on-one with Eric a couple of times. I was able to just kind of throw him aside as I was going back to their quarterback Jeff Blake.

That kind of got my juices going. I think Eric might have said something to me that also got me extra fired up.

It was kind of a perfect storm of circumstances: my daughter's first game, going against a college teammate, Coach LeBeau was figuring out how to use me, and me starting to get comfortable in that position. All those things came together for what I like to say was my breakout party at outside linebacker for the Steelers defense.

I remember the interception I had as well, and their starting running back, Garrison Hearst, blasted me on the return.

I caught it, made a short return, and was kind of looking around trying to figure out where to go, and for whatever reason did not see him coming, and he blasted me.

I ended up fumbling the interception, and we recovered it, but it was an early career interception, and my first career fumble.

It was a great opportunity for the next generation of guys to step up, for Levon to step up, for me to step up and become those types of guys on defense.

## The Aftermath

Brown was a force on the team the remainder of the season, and his sacks came in bunches.

In the team's first playoff game, a home wild card game against the Indianapolis Colts, Brown got to Colts quarterback Jim Harbaugh for three sacks as the Steelers won 42-14.

The 1996 season ended the following week with a tough 28-3 loss to the New England Patriots in the fog in Foxboro.

For Brown, it was also his last game with the Steelers during his first tenure, as that offseason he got a huge free agent offer from the Seattle Seahawks on Valentine's Day 1997.

The deal was the largest in Seahawks history: six years for over $30 million with $7 million guaranteed.

That October afternoon when Brown recorded his huge game for the Steelers against the Bengals was bittersweet, as it started his upward trend to eventually leaving the team that took a chance on him in the second round in 1993.

"From a Steelers perspective and a Steelers fan's perspective, that game kind of became my coming out party, and I continued to play well the rest of the season. I played so well the Steelers could no longer afford to keep me," Brown said.

"That game allowed me to break out on a national scale. It allowed me that offseason to get a huge contract from the Seahawks, but it also ended that recognition as a Steeler, and made me an underrated linebacker for the rest of my career."

Brown did have a successful run with the Seahawks, going to the Pro Bowl in both 1998 and 1999, and amassing 48 sacks during his eight seasons in Seattle.

He also put up 744 total tackles with the Seahawks, had 13 fumble recoveries, and returned three fumble returns for touchdowns.

The linebacker did come full circle, returning to the Steelers in 2006 for eight games, which came in between two stints with the New England Patriots.

As much as Brown was able to have a successful NFL career playing for fifteen seasons before retiring in 2007, he knows that it was his first four-year tenure with the Steelers that laid the groundwork for the rest of his career.

"It was unfortunate. I would have loved to have stayed a Steeler, to be a Steeler linebacker is special. You see a Steelers linebacker in the Pro Bowl virtually every year just because of the style they play," Brown said.

"When you think of Pittsburgh Steelers you think of linebackers, you think of Hall of Fame linebackers, so I certainly missed that way of people looking at me when I went to Seattle.

"I continued to make Pro Bowls and play well, but I didn't get the recognition that my play deserved, and I would have been a lot more recognized if I would have remained a Steeler."

Brown's post-NFL career saw him operate a successful reptile business, one that thrives to this day as he also does some work in broadcasting, a profession that has seen him able to display more of his personality.

He still recognizes, despite it being almost twenty years since his breakout season, that his time with the Steelers was one of the most special times in his life.

"You're also a Steeler, a part of an amazing tradition. You're part of an amazing organization, an amazing community," Brown said.

"The Steelers are bigger than just a football team, they are iconic to that city, and that's how it all ties together."

# CHAPTER 15

# THOM DORNBROOK

**Offensive Lineman 1978–1979**

**September 23, 1979 vs Baltimore Colts at Three Rivers Stadium**

**PITTSBURGH STEELERS 17 - BALTIMORE COLTS 13**

In the course of the 1970s Pittsburgh Steelers dynasty of winning four Super Bowls, there were plenty of players that came and went without a bust in the Pro Football Hall of Fame or even accolades that go along with many Steeler legends.

For one player, just being able to play with the likes of Hall of Famers "Mean" Joe Greene, Jack Lambert, Mike Webster, and Terry Bradshaw was enough to satisfy his NFL dreams.

That player was former Steelers offensive lineman Thom Dornbrook, who played with the black and gold for two seasons in 1978 and 1979.

"I think the dream come true was just the opportunity to play in Pittsburgh," Dornbrook said. "Everything else was gravy."

Dornbrook was born in Pittsburgh in 1956, and played at North Hills High School, the home of fellow NFL players like Washington Redskins linebacker LaVar Arrington and Buffalo Bills defensive back Mark Kelso.

Dornbrook was a starter at the University of Kentucky before waiting for a chance to play for an NFL team.

It just so happened that the team he was able to get a tryout with was the one that played in the city where he was born.

"I went to a tryout mid-to-late June, made the team in 1978, played four games that season, and in 1979 played in all 16 games," Dornbrook said.

When he joined the Steelers in the 1978 season, he played as a backup offensive lineman at both guard and center, and even had the role of handling the teams long snapping duties.

"You had to do all that stuff, you had to make your value anyway you can back then," Dornbrook said.

While not many Steelers fans knew much about Dornbrook, right away he was in the headlines, but not exactly for the right reasons, getting into a brawl on day one with a future Hall of Famer.

"If you look up the Pittsburgh Post-Gazette the first day I was in practice they had a picture of me and Jack Lambert rolling around and you couldn't tell who was who because there was so much dust and we were in a fight," Dornbrook said.

"The way they stopped fights back then is they got the offensive and defensive linemen out there and they just jumped on top of you and you can't punch anybody when you have two tons of people on top of you."

The lineman ended the 1978 season on injured reserve, but was able to learn quite a bit that first season with the Steelers as they made and won their third Super Bowl, topping the Dallas Cowboys in a classic 35-31 win in Super Bowl XIII.

The following year Dornbrook appeared in all 16 games for the Steelers, playing alongside a line that was anchored by Hall of Fame center Mike Webster.

While Dornbrook and Webster had a good on-and off-field relationship, Dornbrook had a rather interesting relationship with Steelers head coach Chuck Noll, a coach and person that wasn't exactly easy to get to know back in those days.

"I think it sums it up the time we went to San Diego and I sat next to him on the bus, and we were talking about tortoises on the side of the road," Dornbrook recalled.

"We played Cincinnati down in Cincinnati and we got beat down there, and Chuck was so mad he took his own plane back," Dornbrook said.

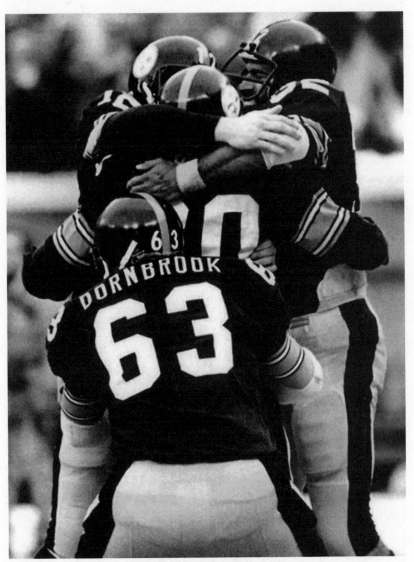

*Courtesy of the Pittsburgh Steelers*

# Notes on Thom Dornbrook

| | |
|---|---|
| **Years Played:** | 1978–1979 |
| **Position:** | Offensive Lineman |
| **Height:** | 6'2" |
| **Weight:** | 240 |
| **Hometown:** | Berea, Ohio |
| **Current Residence:** | Medina, Ohio |
| **Occupation:** | Owns a company that sells roofing materials |
| **Accomplishments:** | Undrafted free agent Center and Guard who played on the Steelers for two seasons in 1978 and 1979. Earned a Super Bowl ring when the Steelers defeated the Los Angeles Rams in Super Bowl XIV in the 1979 season. Went to the Miami Dolphins in the 1980 season after the Steelers attempted to get him through waivers and he was claimed by Miami. Tried to get back with the Steelers in the 1982 season but was cut a week into training camp. Moved to the USFL (United States Football League) and earned a championship with the Michigan Panthers, where he was the starting center in the 1983 season. Played for the Panthers in 1983 and 1984 seasons, and moved to play for the Orlando Renegades for the 1984 and 1985 seasons before his football career ended. |
| **Nickname:** | None |
| **The Game:** | Pittsburgh Steelers vs Baltimore Colts in Pittsburgh, Pennsylvania September 23, 1979 |

"The next meeting we had, which was usually a film session on Tuesday, we had a team meeting before that and we were all sitting there and Chuck comes out and says, 'Look at the guy next to you, the guy next to him has to do better, or there's going to be another guy standing up here.'

"That's the way the pecking order goes in the NFL, you get to learn the politics real fast, and if you don't learn them you're not going to be there real long," Dornbrook said.

The backup offensive lineman got plenty of chances to be educated on the ways of the NFL back in those two seasons with the Steelers, and recalls with fondness a start with the team during their 1979 Super Bowl season against the Baltimore Colts.

## The Game

*By Thom Dornbrook*

My first start of my career was against the Baltimore Colts somewhat early in the 1979 season. We were 3-0 coming off Super Bowl XIII, but we also had a number of injuries, as well.

I knew I was going to start that week on Tuesday as we had guys on the line banged up and Rollie Dotsch, my position coach, told me I was the guy.

I was a big film buff, Mike Webster and I use to lay on the floor and smoke cigars and watch films all the time, and we spent a lot of time that week on film to get ready.

If you just went into the halls where there was Art Rooney's office, he had a whole box of cigars sitting there. He would always say, "Hey if you want one, take one." He walked around all the time, he was at practice now and then, he was just a very funny guy.

So Baltimore had a tough season in 1979, they only won five games, but they still had a pretty good defensive line.

I recall early on in the game I was stuffed on this one run play, and this guy, Mike Barnes—a Pro Bowl defensive tackle—made the tackle.

Chuck called me over to the sideline and said, "Your foot was in the air before you made contact, that's why you got beat. Get your foot down on the ground." That's how detailed Chuck was.

I got my foot down the rest of the game, and never had another problem.

Most of that game I played against Barnes, and he was a really good defensive tackle for a number of years. He made the Pro Bowl in 1978.

I think I handled it pretty well. He beat me a couple of times but after that the rest of the game I was able to hold my own against him.

We won the game 17-13. We really didn't have any major problems handling their defense, and they had a very good defense.

## The Aftermath

The win over the Colts put the Steelers at 4-0, and they would go through the regular season with relative ease, finishing 1979 at 12-4, with Dornbrook appearing in all sixteen games.

The playoffs saw them dominate the Miami Dolphins 34-14, and then in a nip and tuck AFC Title Game, they beat the rival Houston Oilers 24-14 for the right to return to their second straight Super Bowl.

It was in the Super Bowl that Dornbrook had another memorable NFL moment.

"I got to play goal line in the Super Bowl against the Los Angeles Rams. I knocked a guy into the end zone and Franco [Harris] ran behind me and scored a touchdown," Dornbrook recalls.

"The playoff runs and the Super Bowl—it was intense, it was very intense," Dornbrook said. "Everyone learned to turn up the dial full go, and it was a 'let's do this thing,' attitude, never let up.

"We really had to turn it up against the Rams in Super Bowl XIV. They came out smoking against us in the first half. We went into the locker room and Joe [Greene] threw his helmet across the room and shouted obscenities at us."

The motivation must have paid off. The Steelers, who trailed 13-10 at halftime and 19-17 at the end of three quarters, rallied for two fourth-quarter touchdowns, including Harris' plunge past Dornbrook, to win 31-17.

The following season Dornbrook started the season with the Steelers, but fell into a tricky situation after he was injured, which ended his Steelers career.

"Steve Corson had gotten hurt, Sam Davis couldn't play, I was on injured reserve, and they were trying to bring me back off of it, and the only way to do it back then was through the waiver wire," Dornbrook remembers.

"So I was practicing to play against the Miami Dolphins that week, and Chuck said they needed me to play. So he said we're going to take a chance and put you on waivers. So I was out practicing on Friday, Thursday was Thanksgiving so the league office was closed for forty-eight hours. One of the girls came up from the office and told me that I had a telephone call that I had to take.

"I was like 'Really, that's the first time that's ever happened.' So I went into the office of the Steelers. I still had all my gear on and I picked up the phone and it was Don Shula, and he said, 'Welcome to the Miami Dolphins, we're flying in tonight, meet us in the locker room.'

"I took all my stuff out of my locker and moved it down to the visitor's locker room and went through all the sessions with them, and on Sunday played against Joe Greene who I practiced against every day for the last few years.

"It was pretty emotional, but you have to keep that all in check. Offensive linemen have always been taught to be cold and calculating."

Dornbrook appeared in four games in 1980 with the Dolphins, and then went on to play in the USFL (United States Football League) for two seasons with the Michigan Panthers. He was a part of the USFL Championship as the starting center for the Panthers in 1983.

His football career ended following a stint with the Orlando Renegades of the USFL in 1985. Dornbrook owns his own company now, selling roofing materials in Medina, Ohio.

# CHAPTER 16

# MARK BRUENER

### Tight End 1995–2003

#### September 12, 1999 vs Cleveland Browns at
#### Cleveland Browns Stadium

### PITTSBURGH STEELERS 43 - CLEVELAND BROWNS 0

Playing tight end in the city of Pittsburgh has never exactly been a glamourous job. Most of the time, tight ends in Pittsburgh have one job, which is to block and help running backs find room to run.

The Steelers went years without a big name impact tight end. That trend ended in 1990 when the team spent their first-round pick on 6-foot-5, 280-pound beast Eric Green.

For four seasons Green was a terror for opposing teams, and once he hit free agency he took off for what he felt was greener pastures in Miami to play for the Dolphins.

In 1995 the Steelers used another first-round pick on a tight end, taking University of Washington TE Mark Bruener with the 27th overall pick.

For nine seasons, Bruener was a reliable, selfless player, always willing to do what it took to help the team win, blocking or snagging passes.

His best season wound up being his rookie year as the Steelers advanced to Super Bowl XXX. That year he caught what would end up being a career-high 26 passes.

AP Photo/Duane Burleson

# Notes on Mark Bruener

**Years Played:** 1978–1979

**Position:** Tight End

**Height:** 6'2"

**Weight:** 240

**Hometown:** Aberdeen, Washington

**Current Residence:** Aberdeen, Washington

**Occupation:** College Scout for the Pittsburgh Steelers

**Accomplishments:** Steelers first-round pick in 1995, started on the team that lost to the Dallas Cowboys 27-17 in Super Bowl XXX. Starred for four seasons at the University of Washington, where he caught 90 passes in his four years with four touchdowns. Played fourteen seasons in the NFL, nine with the Steelers (1995–2003) and five with the Houston Texans (2003–2008). Caught 152 career passes in the NFL, with 18 touchdowns including a career-high six in 1997 when the Steelers advanced to the AFC Title Game vs the Denver Broncos. Formerly served on the NFL Players Association Executive Committee. Was hired by the Steelers in September of 2010 as a college scout, and travels throughout the west coast from his home in the state of Washington watching players as they prepare for a possible NFL future.

**Nickname:** None

**The Game:** Pittsburgh Steelers vs Cleveland Browns in Cleveland, Ohio
September 12, 1999

"A lot of times when you are evaluating or making an opinion on the tight end position, you're looking at stats or the number of receptions," Bruener said.

"Tony Gonzalez is the all-time leader for receptions for the tight end position. Rob Gronkowski is known as one of the best tight ends in the league currently, because of his receiving skills and how much he can take advantage of a mismatch with a safety or a linebacker covering him."

Bruener's job was not like that of Gonzalez or Gronkowski, his job was to make sure running backs saw daylight once they got the ball.

It came as no surprise to see the Steelers at or near the top of the NFL rushing each season, with Jerome Bettis wearing down teams with his size and strength, and Bruener opening holes for him.

Bruener was a class act, a good teammate and someone's play that you never had to worry about on the field, nor his conduct off of it.

# The Game

*By Mark Bruener*

There was a game I felt like, as far as blocking goes, that we really imposed our will, and that game was the Cleveland game in 1999 when they opened up their new stadium.

Drew Carey was there, fans were going crazy before the game yelling, "Cleveland Rocks," and there was a number of things in that game that really stand out to me.

Against the defensive ends and the defensive line that we were facing, we had the ability that night to really just impose our will on them. We were basically able to run at will on those guys.

Jerome Bettis had 89 yards rushing, and overall as a team we put up over 200 yards on the ground, and it was one of those things where you could literally see the defeat in their eyes, and it you could see their look like, "I'm tired of getting beat by these guys." The number of times that I was blocking a guy downfield, and literally imposing my own individual will on him, to me was very, very satisfying.

Chris Palmer was the Browns head coach at the time. Since they were more or less an expansion team, what we had to do to prepare for them was look back at tape of when Palmer was the offensive coordinator of Jacksonville to see the type of offense they would play. Bob Slowik was their defensive coordinator and we looked back at tape when he was running the defense in his previous job in Chicago to prepare for what they would be running.

You have a little tape of them in the preseason, and they won the Hall of Fame game, but really no one really prepares for that preseason game.

The game you watch and take things from is the third preseason game, and you're able to get a glimpse of what that opponent is going to be like through some of the film, as well as the coaches that are there and the style of offense and defense they ran with their previous teams.

I will say, however, that the rivalry itself between the two cities and the two teams was really what I think was the strong common denominator. It was easy to get up motivation for the game and find a way to want to beat these guys.

You have a brand new stadium and a brand new team, and there was a team there before they left, so it wasn't like there hadn't been football there before, so all that excitement was extremely easy for us to get motivated.

I remember two players for them, Mike McCrary and Rob Burnett, that played for Cleveland that to me were outstanding football players.

The number of individual battles that I got into with Rob Burnett was huge. I knew the week leading up to that game it was going to be an absolute slugfest, from their defense as a whole as well as that individual battle.

There was a game my rookie year, before Cleveland moved to Baltimore following the 1995 season, and I was in a play and Burnett actually ripped my helmet off.

I continued on the play, and he gave me a couple of blows to the head without my helmet on. I had a pretty good laceration on my face.

When you're in the heat of the moment you don't actually know what you look like. I remember sitting on the bench and one of my teammates goes, "God, man, what happened to your face, you're all beat up!" I said, "I don't know, all I know is I got my helmet ripped off a couple of plays ago." I remember looking in the mirror after the game and I had all kinds of red welts and things on my face.

The competitive respect that I had for Rob Burnett and Mike McCrary throughout all those years was immense.

Those were the games, the memorable games that I knew going in were going to be just a slugfest.

The emotion of the team going into that game that opening night was like, "Look, we have this brand new stadium, it's the Cleveland Browns and their kind of welcome back party," and for us to kind of annihilate those guys, that to me was a big part of the game.

As far as Burnett and McCrary go, now that we are all retired, to be able to catch up with those guys, and talk to them and reminisce a little bit, it's quite nice, it really is.

You have that respect as a player and then when you get to talk to them again as a former player, that respect actually grows.

I have a lot of games throughout my career that I could make reference to, but that to me was one of the games, especially with the rivalry situation, that really, really made a lasting impression on me.

## The Aftermath

While the 1999 season got off to a great start for the Steelers with their dominating win over their rivals in Cleveland, it was one of the few bright spots of the season.

The team had arguably the worst season in the Bill Cowher era, going 6-10 and finishing fourth in the crowded six-team AFC Central.

The 1999 Steelers started 2-0, then dropped their next three, and then won three straight to sit at 5-3 entering a Week 10 game at home against the same Browns team they had beaten on opening night by 43 points.

What happened that day was a cruel reminder of just how meaningless games earlier in the year are if you come in overconfident.

The Steelers came into the second meeting with the Browns two touchdown favorites, only to be stunned by the one-win Browns at the time, 16-15.

The moment Phil Dawson's 39-yard field goal sailed through the uprights to give Cleveland the win, the Steelers season never really recovered.

The team lost six in a row, winning just one more time the entire season, a snowy day at home against the Carolina Panthers 30-20 on December 26.

Bruener acknowledged how the loss to the Browns was a major setback, as well as how impactful losing to a rival is.

"When you are talking about the rivalry, it's one of those things where you throw out the records," Bruener said. "You are easily going to get up for that game, the rivalry is very, very strong within those two teams."

Bruener had a solid nine seasons with the black and gold, pulling in 137 catches for 1,197 yards and 16 touchdowns.

He left the Steelers following the 2003 season, and played five more years in the league, all of which were spent with the Houston Texans.

His career concluded after 2008, ending his NFL days playing in 189 games with 152 catches and 18 scores.

Bruener is a family man, living out in the state of Washington with his wife and five children, three sons, and two daughters.

He also remains in the game, as a college scout for the team that drafted him, the Steelers.

Bruener spends a majority of his time scouting colleges out on the west coast. His job is to watch players, and see if they have what it takes to make a successful player in the NFL, the place he called home for fourteen years.

# CHAPTER 17

# MIKE LOGAN

### Safety 2001–2006

#### January 5, 2003 vs Cleveland Browns at Heinz Field

### PITTSBURGH STEELERS 36 - CLEVELAND BROWNS 33

Mike Logan was a home grown player who reached his dream of playing for the team he grew up watching in Pittsburgh.

Logan came to the Steelers as a free agent in 2001 after a four-year stint with the Jacksonville Jaguars, who drafted Logan in the second round of the 1997 draft.

The safety played high school ball at local McKeesport Arena High School in McKeesport, PA, and then went to West Virginia and started all four years at the corner position, as well as shined as a return man during his time there from 1993 to 1996.

When he hit free agency in 2001, Logan took less money to come to Pittsburgh to play for the team that he grew up idolizing. He also wanted to live out a dream playing in the Super Bowl for his hometown team.

He lived that dream in 2005 when the team won Super Bowl XL, but had to go through a gruesome injury before he was able to collect that ring.

Logan was part of one of the most memorable wins in the history of the Steelers, a game in which they trailed for over fifty-nine minutes before rallying to beat the Cleveland Browns 36-33 in the 2002 AFC Wild Card Game at Heinz Field.

AP Photo/Gary Tramontina

## Notes on Mike Logan

**Years Played:** 2001–2006

**Position:** Safety

**Height:** 6'0"

**Weight:** 212

**Hometown:** Pittsburgh, Pennsylvania

**Current Residence:** Pittsburgh, Pennsylvania

**Occupation:** Teaches life skills and mentoring at Obama Academy and University Prep in the Pittsburgh area, and local Radio Personality

**Accomplishments:** Drafted in the second round, 50th overall, by the Jacksonville Jaguars in the 1997 NFL Draft. Before that played his college ball at McKeesport Area High School in PA, where he played under WPIAL famed Coach George Smith. Played his college ball at West Virginia University. Earned the starting free safety job in Jacksonville in his third season. Inked with the Steelers in 2001, and was on the team when they won the Super Bowl in 2005 defeating the Seattle Seahawks in Super Bowl XL. Played in 116 career games over ten seasons, starting twenty-eight games. He recorded five interceptions and recovered seven fumbles in his ten seasons. Had a career-high 94 tackles and a sack in the 2003 season.

**Nickname:** None

**The Game:** Pittsburgh Steelers vs Cleveland Browns in Pittsburgh, Pennsylvania
January 5, 2003

The game was bittersweet for Logan, who tore up his knee on a key third-quarter interception with the Steelers already down 17 points and the Browns driving at the Steelers' 32.

The play symbolized the career for Logan, a play in which he gave his all and put his body on the line for the good of the team.

He lived out his dream playing for the Steelers, winning a title, and still to this day talking Steelers football and also helping youth in the Pittsburgh area.

# The Game
*By Mike Logan*

It was a playoff game; to me it was one of the most exciting games of my career during the ten years that I played.

Being able to come back and get that playoff victory in the AFC Wild Card after being down at one point 17 points, it was very, very special to me.

We were definitely confident, without a doubt. It sounds cliché, but when you look at your schedule at the beginning of the year and with us playing in the division that we play in, you kind of know what games are going to be hard-fought games. Some of those games that you are going to take for granted, you're already going to circle and put in the win column.

The Cleveland Browns were one of those opponents we felt like we had their number. Anytime we played them, despite how we prepared we felt like we were going to get the victory.

Now I'm not saying that we weren't going to have to come out and show up and play, but we always felt like there was an opportunity for us to go out and beat the Cleveland Browns no matter how the game unfolded.

For this particular game, it was an AFC Wild Card Game, so we knew that they were going to prepare. They were going to come in hyped; they were thinking upset.

For us, as a team who wore that aura about who we are when we played the Cleveland Browns, we thought we were going to win.

I won't go so far as to say we were talking about it when it came to the game plan, but from the time I played for the Pittsburgh Steelers and we lined up to play the Cleveland Browns, we felt there was a greater percentage for us to beat them.

That game was no different. I would imagine it was no different for us as far as the mentality in preparation for us to go out and beat the Cleveland Browns, whether it was a regular season game, whether both of us were not going to make the playoffs, or if it was a wild card, which it was.

They jumped out to a big lead, and I remember being in shock. Kelly Holcomb, who played for them at quarterback, was really shredding up our secondary.

Now we were very confident as we always were as the Pittsburgh Steelers because our game plan was set on stopping the run.

But we did have some weaknesses in our secondary. At the time I was playing inconsistently, I really was, and I really struggled in that game.

Quincy Morgan was one of their receivers, as was Dennis Northcutt. They had some shifty receivers, and they were able to find some open space in our secondary. They were able to sit down and make some plays.

I recall in that game they beat us on a real deep pass for a big play, and remember Dick LeBeau emphasized not giving up the big play. We were kind of in shock, saying, "This guy is having some success against us." Whenever we prepared to play an inexperienced quarterback, whether he was a rookie or a player who hadn't been in the NFL for a long time, we were able to pin our ears back and really take advantage of that zone blitz scheme that we ran in Pittsburgh.

We were ready to pin our ears back, thinking we could get some pressure on him, really shake him up with our disguises, assignments, and things like that.

He really never seemed rattled and wasn't fazed by the things we were throwing at him. I think it was very evident by halftime because he had a pretty good first half in that game against us.

In the second half we were down, and we knew that we had to create a turnover. Everybody was going to be that guy. Everyone was saying "We're going to create a turnover, somehow, someway." In the back of my mind, I was just thinking I want to go out and play consistent, and if I make the big play so be it. Lo and behold, I was in the right place at the right time, and I was able to snag the ball.

Instantly when I snagged the ball and came down after the reception, I knew that I had blown my knee out. I actually felt something, I don't know if it was a pop or snap, but something just didn't feel right.

My adrenaline was flowing so high, at the time I had a couple interceptions in my career, but when you intercept a pass you never really think about what you're doing at that time. But I knew exactly at that moment how big of an impact that play was, and how significant that play was going to be if we were going to be able to come back.

In a split second I just knew that was going to be a spark for us, so with all that emotion for me thinking about that moment, I decided to try and run that interception back and try and make something happen, with my leg already in pain.

So I was just running, and I remember running across the field, and I remember DeShea Townsend yelling at me to pitch the ball back, because we had a secondary of guys that all wanted to be return men.

I was looking at him thinking, "I'm going to get as far as I can with this ball," and I could feel my leg really being unstable, and as I tried to plant in the turf and change direction to go across the field, I was able to do it but I knew that my knee wasn't stable.

I want to say I ran a full 53 yards across the field sideline to sideline and I finally went down, but then after the game I saw I ran about 10 yards.

It was just one of those things, but right then I knew that something pretty significant had happened to my knee. But when I went to the sideline I wanted to go back in. I told the training staff I did something to my knee, I told them my knee gave out.

I tried to plant in that horrible Heinz Field turf we had at that time, the muck and mud as we use to call it, and it just came up from under me. I wasn't able to plant, and it was probably due to how bad the field conditions were at the time.

Anytime you have wet and slippery conditions, the more running backs have the ball, the better chance they are going to have at creating a turnover. We had that in our mindset to go out and try and strip the ball away, but the Browns were having a lot of success throwing the ball early. We knew they were going to continue to do it.

After the interception I tried to brace up and tried to hide from Dr. Bradley, who was our surgeon, to try and not get checked out. When he found me and was able to get me on that table to check me out, he was testing my range of motion, and I was doing my best to hide the pain, but at the end of the day the damage was tremendous.

I did a lot of things to that knee on that particular play, and I wasn't able to come back into the game.

I remember going into the locker room, and Dr. Bradley and the medical staff of the Steelers telling me that my day was over. Of course I was devastated, but there was a game to play. I went into the locker room, but I came back out on the field.

I was getting updates on the game, and still felt like we had an opportunity to come back, and then I was able to go back out on the field and join the rest of my teammates.

When you come back as a team like that from being down, in an emotional state in a playoff game, then your team comes out victorious and guys are coming up to you saying, "Hey, it was your spark and we feel for you man." That was special to me.

I was pretty good friends with Chris Fuamatu-Ma'afala, who scored the winning touchdown, and being able to celebrate with him and his family afterwards was just outstanding.

Even though I knew I wouldn't be able to go on and continue our playoff journey with them, it was special. It was a really special moment for me, and that's why I will always remember that game.

## The Aftermath

The injury to Logan was extensive, as he had a slightly torn LCL, a sprained MCL, a torn meniscus, a microfracture, and posterior reconstruction. "I basically did everything to my knee except tear the ACL," Logan said.

The safety watched the following week from his basement, which he turned into a theater room, as the Steelers nearly upset the favored Tennessee Titans on the road, falling in the end in the AFC Divisional Playoff Game 34-31 in overtime.

"I was uncomfortable not only from my surgery and my rehab, but from the way the game was going and the results of that game," Logan said. "I wasn't a pleasant person to be around."

Despite the loss the following week, the Steelers AFC Wild Card win over the Browns remains one of, if not the most memorable comeback in Steelers playoff history.

The team had to overcome Browns backup QB Kelly Holcomb's monster day in which he threw for 429 yards and three touchdowns.

It was the one mistake that he made which seemed to turn the game around though, as Logan's pick of Holcomb not only stopped a Browns drive, but started a Steelers comeback after the team at one point trailed in the third quarter 24-7.

Logan returned to the Steelers after the surgery, missing a little of the following training camp for the Steelers in 2003, but finished that season playing in all sixteen games and putting up a career-high 93 tackles.

He stayed with the Steelers for the next three seasons, earning a Super Bowl ring with the team when they beat the Seattle Seahawks in the 2005 season in Super Bowl XL.

He walked away from the game prior to the 2007 season, ending his career playing in Super Bowl XL.

Logan now plays the part of an educator, teaching life skills and mentoring at Obama Academy and University Prep in the Pittsburgh area.

He also still follows and talks Steelers football on a weekly basis, doing a show on the *Pittsburgh Tribune's* website, and also does commentary for West Virginia for Root Sports, and does color commentary for the Arena League's Pittsburgh Power.

# CHAPTER 18

# ANDY RUSSELL

### Linebacker 1963–1976
### September 15, 1963 vs Philadelphia Eagles at Franklin Field
### PITTSBURGH STEELERS 21 - PHILADELPHIA EAGLES 21

While the ending of Andy Russell's Pittsburgh Steelers career was one filled with Super Bowls and plenty of winning, the beginning of his career began very differently.

Russell grew up in New York before moving to St. Louis, where he went to Ladue High School, playing end. In his junior and senior years he played fullback and linebacker, and along the way earned all-state honors.

He went to college at Missouri, and was picked by the Steelers in the sixteenth round of the 1963 NFL Draft, not exactly a high-profile pick for a player who went on to play thirteen NFL seasons.

Russell absorbed losing, a lot of losing in the first nine years of his thirteen seasons playing with the black and gold. In those first nine years, the Steelers went 36-83-6, with the worst season coming in 1969, Chuck Noll's first year.

That season the club went 1-13, and many felt it was a case of "here we go again" until suddenly with a couple quality drafts, the Steelers quickly became winners.

It started with an "Immaculate Reception" in 1972, and two years later the club found themselves in the Super Bowl, topping the Minnesota Vikings 16-6.

AP Photo

# Notes on Andy Russell

| | |
|---|---|
| **Years Played:** | 1963–1976 |
| **Position:** | Linebacker |
| **Height:** | 6'2" |
| **Weight:** | 225 |
| **Hometown:** | Detroit, Michigan |
| **Current Residence:** | Pittsburgh, Pennsylvania |
| **Occupation:** | Managing Partner at Laurel Mountain Partners in Pittsburgh |
| **Accomplishments:** | Drafted in the sixteenth round, 220nd pick overall in the 1963 Draft. All-Pro rookie team in 1963, All-Pro or All-Conference seven years, seven Pro Bowls (the only linebacker in the NFL to play six consecutive Pro Bowls between 1971–1976). Was the Steelers Team Captain for ten years. Earned a degree in economics at the University of Missouri. Left the team at one point for the Army to fulfill ROTC commitments from Missouri. Steelers MVP in 1971. Inducted into the Pennsylvania Hall of Fame, the University of Missouri Hall of Fame, the Missouri State Hall of Fame, and the Pittsburgh Pro Football Hall of Fame. Played in 186 games in the NFL, Military, College, and High School, never missing a game in his football career. Played on two Steelers Super Bowl teams, 1975 and 1976 before retiring and going into business. |
| **Nickname:** | None |
| **The Game:** | Pittsburgh Steelers vs Philadelphia Eagles in Philadelphia, Pennsylvania September 15, 1963 |

Before all that, Russell wasn't even sure he would make the team. In 1963 the Steelers coach was Buddy Parker. He was known for not liking young players, trading away a lot of his picks for older players who he trusted more.

"He had traded away the first seven draft choices," Russell said of Parker. "The theoretical first round was a guy named Frank Atkinson, who was drafted in the eighth round."

Russell, though a sixteenth-round pick, made the team, and in his first pro game was able to make enough of an impact to pave the way for a successful career that eventually saw him part of two Super Bowl title teams.

# The Game
*By Andy Russell*

It's kind of a funny story. My rookie year was 1963, and we almost won the championship that year. Our coach that season was Buddy Parker, and Parker hated rookies.

He told us, "I hate rookies, rookies lose games, if it was up to me I would cut all of you, but The Chief (Art Rooney) wants me to keep a couple of you." So there I was thinking that I would be lucky just to make that team, let alone play. So I made the team, but I was just thinking I'd end up playing special teams, kickoffs and punts and things like that.

I was thinking to myself I'd play one year, and then I had to go in the military for two years to serve as a Lieutenant in Germany.

I thought well, then I will get back from the military and get my MBA and go to work. I'd have a one-year NFL experience.

So we opened the 1963 season, we played the Philadelphia Eagles in Philadelphia in our first game.

The first quarter of that game, John Reger, the veteran linebacker, went down in front of our Steelers bench with a massive concussion, and swallowed his tongue.

The Steeler couldn't find the screw that opens your mouth. Obviously he was unconscious and he was not going to open his mouth, so we couldn't talk to him.

So he was starting to turn blue. He was dying, because he couldn't breathe. I ran out there and grabbed the doctor. He couldn't get his mouth open, so then he took this pair of scissors, and chopped Reger's teeth out.

Reger got his front teeth chipped out, they got his tongue out, and he was taken away in an ambulance.

Mind you I was not even the first backup, I was the second backup at linebacker. The first backup was a big guy, 6'4", 240 pounds, Bob Schmitz.

Schmitz went in to back up Reger, and the first play he was in there he broke his ankle and they took him off on a stretcher.

So they go, "Russell get in there," and I was thinking, "I'm not so sure I even want to play in this game." I remember being a rookie that was running around like his head was cut off during that game, trying to make a play, trying to survive.

I didn't play that well in my opinion that day I felt like I made too many mistakes. They kept starting me and I kept the job the rest of the year.

I made the All-Pro rookie team, so I was thrilled. To me, that was more meaningful than making All-American, which I didn't do.

Jon Reger came back six or seven weeks later, but they released George Tarasovic who played on the other side, and he took George's place.

It was the big break that every young player would like to have. I ended up making the All-Pro rookie team and it was a great experience. I was a lucky guy.

It was probably the most meaningful game I ever played in.

## The Aftermath

Early on in his career, Russell was one of the few bright spots on the Steelers roster. The team did have a successful year in 1963, as the club went 7-4-3.

Yes, three ties, something you would likely never see in the NFL today.

"We had a lot of ties that year, three of them, and back in those days they didn't have a way to break ties," Russell said.

One of those ties included the opener in Philadelphia when Russell made his NFL debut in a position that he would stay at for the next thirteen seasons.

The season saw the Steelers sitting at 4-3-1 entering a Week 9 contest with the Cleveland Browns. Pittsburgh won the game in a 9-7 after trailing 7-0, they got a safety and a fourth-quarter touchdown to win the game.

From there they would go 2-0-2 to set up a huge game in Week 14.

"We played the New York Giants in the final game of that season at Yankee Stadium. If we would have won that game we would have been in the game that today is known as the Super Bowl," Russell said.

"Back then it was known as the NFL Championship Game, in those days there were only twelve teams in the NFL, now of course there are thirty-two."

The Steelers had defeated the Giants earlier in the season 31-0 in Week 2, but on this day at Yankee Stadium the Giants got revenge, beating the Steelers 33-17 to advance to the NFL Title Game. A game they would lose to the Chicago Bears, 14-10.

Russell prospered despite the Steelers struggling, making the Pro Bowl in 1968 for the first time. It was that offseason he had an interesting first meeting with new head coach Chuck Noll.

"He called me in that offseason and I went over to see him," Russell recalls.

"I was so naïve I thought he was going to compliment me for making my first Pro Bowl, and instead he said, 'I don't like the way you play.'

"He told me, 'You're too out of control, you're too aggressive, you are trying to make the big play.' I told him, 'Well coach we're losing games, I'm trying to make a play,' to which he told me, 'I'm going to change the way you play, I'll make you a better player in your thirties then you were in your twenties.'"

Noll must have been on to something. Russell went on to make seven Pro Bowls, five of them taking place from ages thirty to thirty-four when he walked away from the game with two Super Bowl rings.

Russell started at one of the linebacker spots for the Steelers in both Super Bowl IX and Super Bowl X, wrapping up a career that saw him named to the Steelers All-Time Team. In 2013 Russell was inducted into the Pittsburgh Pro Football Hall of Fame.

# CHAPTER 19

# DWIGHT STONE

## Wide Receiver 1987–1994

### September 1, 1991 vs San Diego Chargers at Three Rivers Stadium
### PITTSBURGH STEELERS 26 - SAN DIEGO CHARGERS 20

The road to the NFL for former Pittsburgh Steelers wide receiver Dwight Stone was not a road normally taken by most NFL players.

Stone was an undrafted free agent, who never played wide receiver until his third season with the franchise in 1989.

He was a speedster, a player who worked hard not only to figure out his new position, but how to play it well and thrive at it.

Before he could even get the chance though, he first had to make the roster of the black and gold out of Middle Tennessee State.

He worked hard that first preseason to try to impress the coaching staff and head coach Chuck Noll. Once preseason was over, he learned the fate of his future from an unlikely source one day sitting in the trainer's room.

"I remember Art Rooney Sr. when I was a rookie, we had just been through preseason and everyone was on pins and needles because we had just been through the last cut," Stone said.

"Me being a rookie I was nervous. With everyone that walks by you're ready to jump because you're thinking, 'This is the one, I'm gone.'

"So I saw Mr. Rooney, and we were at Three Rivers Stadium, and I was in the training room and he was coming in my direction. He walked up to me and said, 'Hey you're Dwight, right?' I said, 'Yes sir.' He said, 'You're the fast one aren't you?'

"I said to him, 'Yes, sir, I am the fast one. I can be the slow one, I can be whatever you need me to be, just let me know.'" Stone laughed when recounting the story. "He said to me, 'Congratulations you made the team.' I was like, 'Wow!'

"I had not heard it from the scouts, I hadn't heard it from the head coach, so when he came over and told me that, I was thinking, 'You're the gentleman with four Super Bowls, you know people galore, yet he came up to me and talked to me and took his time out.' It showed me just how personable he was and that sat very well with me."

Stone in his first year with the Steelers was mostly a special teams player, catching just one pass and getting 17 chances to rush the ball.

It was much of the same in 1988 when he made 11 catches for 196 yards and one score, and ran the ball 40 times for 127 yards.

It was 1989 when the coaches came to Stone and asked him about using his speed more at the receiver position.

While he wasn't thrilled about the change, he went along with it, and that first year caught just seven passes for 92 yards.

Finally things began to click for Stone in year two at the wide out position. In 1990 he caught 19 passes for 332 yards and a score, and had a memorable 90-yard grab in a blowout win over the Denver Broncos.

When 1991 started, which turned out to be Noll's last season, the team was determined to get Stone the ball, and do what they could to get him in space.

It was the first game of the 1991 season that Stone recalls most where the team did just that.

# Notes on Dwight Stone

| | |
|---|---|
| **Years Played:** | 1987–1994 |
| **Position:** | Wide Receiver |
| **Height:** | 6'0" |
| **Weight:** | 191 |
| **Hometown:** | Florala, Alabama |
| **Current Residence:** | Charlotte, North Carolina |
| **Occupation:** | Police Officer |
| **Accomplishments:** | Played fourteen seasons in the NFL, eight with the Steelers, four with the Panthers and his final two with the New York Jets. Played in 216 career games with 52 starts, catching 154 passes for 2,478 yards and 12 touchdowns catches, one rushing. Best season was 1992 under new head coach Bill Cowher when he caught 34 passes for 501 yards and three touchdowns. Started his Steelers career as a running back, making the transition to wide out in 1989. Also returned kicks and punts during NFL career, taking back a kick for a score in 1988 with the Steelers in a December 37–34 win over the Houston Oilers. Best known for his speed, was timed at 4.25 in the 40-yard dash. Played his college ball at Middle Tennessee State University. |
| **Nickname:** | None |
| **The Game:** | Pittsburgh Steelers vs Philadelphia Eagles in Pittsburgh, Pennsylvania September 15, 1963 |

# The Game
*By Dwight Stone*

The game I can recall best was the game in which I caught my first touchdown pass of the season. It went for 89 yards against San Diego to open up the 1991 season at Three Rivers Stadium.

I was making the transition from running back to wide receiver in 1989 and 1990, that's when they wanted to start me playing wide out full-time, and I thought, "Oh man what are they doing?" But I made the transition, and my best year was 1991. I scored five touchdowns that season.

That opening game we were playing well, and we were up big in the fourth quarter. We led the game 19-3, and all of a sudden the Chargers came back and it was 19-13 late in the fourth quarter.

We were backed up in our own end and it was a third down and long play. Our quarterback, Bubby Brister, had just gone down with an injury, and Neil O'Donnell had just come in the game.

There was a timeout, and we needed like 19 yards for a first, so we were basically trying to get out of our own end zone and give our punter some room to punt.

I came out and the play was more or less a screen, and it seemed to take the ball forever to come down in my hands.

I caught it, and the next thing I knew I was running up the sidelines with no one in front of me.

The most important thing about that play was that the catch was good, but if you watch the whole setup, [fellow wide receiver] Louis Lipps blocked three Chargers on that play.

It was like the red sea parting once he threw that block and I thought, "Man this is easy, something has to be wrong with this, something is not right." Sure enough I had open field.

When you look at that play you say, "Man," because of the block. Of course all the guys are ribbing me since I was still a pretty young guy, saying I only score because of the block.

Louis, though, came up laughing and said, "Don't pay no attention to them." The one thing that was funny about that catch was I didn't wear contacts or glasses when I played running back, and the coaches and other guys were all saying, "Hey Dwight why do you wait for the last minute to catch the ball?" I said, "I can't see the ball coming till the last minute." Come to find out I needed contacts, so I went to see a doctor and I thought after, "Man, that ball is clear now!" As a running back I always had people handing the ball off to me, so it really wasn't as important to see, but as a wide receiver it was tough to see the depth of the ball, the perception of the ball.

Also in college you have that little white stripe on the ball, in the pro game you don't.

After I scored the touchdown I threw the ball in the stands, because there were some people there that I knew from Ohio.

I didn't have a clue where they were, but I threw it in the stands anyway, and I went over to the sidelines all happy, and one of guys told me, "Oh man that's going to cost you." I said, "What do you mean?" He said, 'You can't throw the ball into the stands, the NFL is going to fine you.'" Sure enough, we came in the day after the win and Mr. [Dan] Rooney, who now was the owner of the team, said to me, "Dwight, now you know you can't throw the ball in the stands; you get fined by the league for that." I said, "Yes Mr. Rooney, I'm sorry I didn't know that. That's going to be like my whole game check." Mr. Rooney said, "Dwight, don't worry about it; we are going to cover it for you." He told me next time just to hold on to it 'til I got to the sidelines and give it to the people I knew later.

It was another class move by Mr. Rooney. Winning the opener didn't hurt either.

## The Aftermath

1991 was the end of an era for the Steelers, as it was the final year of coaching for Hall of Fame coach Chuck Noll, who walked away following that season.

The team showed signs of being good in 1991, as they sat at 3-2 five games into the season. On a Monday Night against the World Champion New York Giants at home in Week 6, the Steelers fell behind 20-0, before rallying only to fall in the final seconds, 23-20.

The deflating loss started a crushing four-game losing streak that put the team at 3-6 and basically out of the playoff race in the AFC.

The club did recover to win four of their final seven, with Stone having the best season of his career, catching 32 passes for 649 yards and five scores.

Stone lasted with the Steelers three more seasons, starting twenty-eight games over the final three years in Pittsburgh.

Under new coach Bill Cowher in 1992, Stone grabbed 34 passes for 501 yards and three scores, and even ran the ball twelve times for 118 yards.

His last season in Pittsburgh Stone caught a career-high 41 passes for 587 yards and two touchdowns. He again had 12 carries for 121 yards and a score.

Stone played in the NFL for six more seasons, playing through 2000, four seasons with the Carolina Panthers and two with the New York Jets.

While he never found success with the Panthers and Jets like he did with the Steelers, Stone proved his worth in his twelve-year NFL career.

The undrafted free agent's career ended playing in 216 games, catching 154 passes for 2,478 yards and 12 touchdowns. He ran the ball for 596 yards in his career with one touchdown.

His post-NFL career saw Stone take on a completely second profession, as he now plays the role of officer—police officer—in the city of Charlotte, North Carolina.

# CHAPTER 20

# ANDRE
# HASTINGS

### Wide Receiver 1993–1996

#### January 28, 1996 vs Dallas Cowboys at
#### Sun Devil Stadium

### DALLAS COWBOYS 27 - PITTSBURGH STEELERS 17

For a moment in time, Pittsburgh Steelers wide receiver Andre Hastings had an opportunity most in the NFL only dream of, to become a household name in front of millions watching on television around the world.

The chance came on the biggest stage in the National Football League, that being the Super Bowl. On January 28, 1996, the Steelers wide out was on the verge of a historical performance in front of over 95 million television viewers.

Hastings had pulled in 10 catches, and the Steelers had the ball with 4:15 remaining in the fourth quarter, and the black and gold trailed the heavily favored Dallas Cowboys by just three at 20-17.

Following an incomplete pass, quarterback Neil O'Donnell went back to pass, and threw a pass where he felt Hastings would be.

Instead, Hastings ran an inside slant while O'Donnell threw it outside. The result: an interception by eventual Super Bowl MVP Larry Brown who took it back inside the Steelers 10-yard line.

Seconds later, a Cowboys touchdown by Emmitt Smith ended the Steelers' hopes, as well as the hopes of a moment in time for Hastings and the Steelers.

Why did the play go so wrong? No one ever seems to have that answer.

"We kind of all agreed not to talk about it," Hastings said about the play.

Years later, Hastings now goes by the name Orlando, running a dog training business in Arizona. He's still a bubble of energy when he talks about his time with the Steelers and his eight-year NFL career.

"It was fantastic. Even with the draft and stuff I would have liked to have gone higher, but I couldn't have thought of a better place to go," Hastings said. "One of my former college coaches, Bob Harrison, was also my position coach with the Steelers, which could be why I ended up in Pittsburgh. He coached me at Georgia for two years.

"I tell people now there are certain organizations that always win. Other organizations seem to go up and down, but being around people with traditions and winning traditions in Pittsburgh, that's maybe the best thing that happened to me."

At Georgia, Hastings had a solid three-year run, pulling in 124 catches with 13 touchdowns. The Steelers took him in the third round of the 1993 NFL Draft, the 76th pick overall.

When Hastings arrived, the team was built around a fast offensive line that opened up holes for running backs like Barry Foster and Bam Morris.

In 1994 the Steelers went 12-4 in the regular season, with Hastings pulling in 20 passes for 281 yards and two scores.

The team appeared Super Bowl bound when they dispatched their rivals the Cleveland Browns 29-9 in the AFC Divisional Playoff Game.

The following week they met the underdog San Diego Chargers in the AFC Title Game in Pittsburgh, and lost one of the most stunning upsets in franchise history 17-13, a game that still has a sour taste to fans and former players to this day.

"I remember losing that 1994 AFC Championship Game to San Diego when Tony Martin caught that long touchdown over Tim McKyer to give San Diego the lead for good," Hastings recalls.

AP Photo/Bill Sykes

# Notes on Andre Hastings

| | |
|---|---|
| **Years Played:** | 1993–1996 |
| **Position:** | Wide Receiver |
| **Height:** | 6'1" |
| **Weight:** | 190 |
| **Hometown:** | Atlanta, Georgia |
| **Current Residence:** | Charlotte, North Carolina |
| **Occupation:** | Owns a company called "Best in Show" which trains dogs and also serves as a kennel |
| **Accomplishments:** | Was the 1989 USA Today Offensive Player of the Year while at Morrow High School. Played his college ball at Georgia, catching 124 passes for 1,836 yards and 13 touchdowns in three seasons. All-SEC: 1991 (AP 2nd team), 1992 (AP 1st team, Coaches' 1st team). Tied for fourth-highest single season receiving yardage in UGA history. Was drafted by the Steelers in the third-round, 76th pick overall, in the 1993 NFL Draft. Played from 1993 to 2000 with the Steelers, New Orleans Saints, and Tampa Bay Buccaneers. Pulled in 10 catches for 98 yards and returned two punts for 18 yards for the Steelers during the teams' 27-17 loss at Super Bowl XXX. Caught 266 passes for 3,307 yards and 18 touchdowns during NFL career. |
| **Nickname:** | None |
| **The Game:** | Pittsburgh Steelers vs Dallas Cowboys in Tempe, Arizona |
| | January 28, 1996 |

"I can remember watching it like it was in slow motion thinking, 'What is he doing?' as the ball was coming down."

The awful setback to the Chargers in the AFC Title Game seemed to have a hangover the following season.

The Steelers were picked by many to be the AFC representative in Super Bowl XXX, but the season didn't start well at all, as the team after seven games was 3-4 and searching for answers.

The team then went on a run, going to a more wide open offense, with five wide outs with Hastings being one of them.

That season he doubled his 2004 output, with 48 catches for 502 yards and one touchdown. O'Donnell spread the ball around, and it paid off as the team won eight of their last nine games in the regular season.

"We started to really gel in 1995 after we started off slow. We started to get it together. It wasn't about one specific person. On our offense it felt like everyone got a little piece of the pie," Hastings said.

The Steelers topped the Buffalo Bills 40-21 in the AFC Divisional Playoff Game at Three Rivers Stadium, and then in a thriller they beat the Indianapolis Colts 20-16 in the AFC Championship Game.

During that game Hastings pulled in a pass that saved the season, a 4th-and-3 catch with the game on the line late that allowed the eventual Steelers final touchdown drive to stay alive.

The Steelers went on for the win, and then two weeks later Hastings was back in the spotlight as he took the field for Super Bowl XXX in Tempe, Arizona against the Cowboys.

# The Game

*By Andre Hastings*

Super Bowl XXX was just unbelievable for me and for our team. I had a really good game; it seemed like Neil [O'Donnell] was just looking for me all day.

What we were doing was working really well on our offense, and just one way or another, if I got one more catch and I'd tie the Super Bowl record for receptions.

I remember I did have a drop in that game. I separated my clavicle early in the game, and I had a drop when the ball got to me, I had pain. Not to make an excuse for dropping the ball, but it happened and I ended up being one short of the reception record.

I got another catch and we won the game and I could have possibly been the MVP. It would have been even more special since the game was played in Arizona, and I had a home in Arizona at that time.

The Cowboys, that specific team, had been to the Super Bowl before, and of course we had not, so it took a little while for us as a team to settle in.

We started slow, fell behind 13-0 early, and obviously that wasn't the game plan, but it just took us awhile to settle down and get into the game.

Finally we started to get our feet wet. We got that first hit and it was like "boom, boom, boom," and then we finally snapped out of it.

I remember thinking once we got going that we definitely had that game. Our defense was stopping them, you could see them getting frustrated.

One kind of funny moment I remember was playing against [Cowboys Hall of Fame CB] Deion [Sanders]. He, myself, and Rod Woodson all had the same agent, Eugene Parker, and I remember when I was in high school Deion came to one of my high school football games, so that's the first time I got to meet him.

During the game I made a catch over the middle, and I started to turn up field and Deion was the first person there to try to make the tackle. I made him miss, and he came up to me and we were laughing back and forth.

We seemed to have a special comradery there as well as outside of football, and during all the hoopla of the biggest game of the season it was a special moment.

There was no reason I didn't think we were not going to win that game, then that last interception came. At that moment all we were thinking was let's keep moving the ball, let's get down and score points.

We knew they were not going to score on our defense again. When that pick happened, it was surreal almost, like it wasn't real, like it couldn't really have just happened.

That's part of sports, just coming up short. But looking back I can say there's plenty of other teams and other players that had never gotten the chance to even be there.

## The Aftermath

The loss marked the end of a run for the Steelers. They lost their starting quarterback in O'Donnell that offseason, as he left the team to sign as a free agent with the New York Jets.

In 1996 Hastings turned into one of the most productive wide outs in the game, pulling in 72 passes that season for 739 yards and six touchdowns, all career highs.

A lot of the success Hastings had he credits to how the Steelers used him, and the system of quarterbacks he was able to play under.

"I look back now and I watch other teams and what many don't realize is there's two or three athletes that are superior athletes, and everyone else is actually pretty much close," Hastings said.

"It's all about the system, and like I said, for me going to Pittsburgh it was about the team and the positions the organization put me in. It could have been totally different if I would have went somewhere else.

"I always can remember naming our quarterbacks when I was in Pittsburgh, players like Mike Tomczak, Kordell Stewart, and Neil O'Donnell.

"Then when I left Pittsburgh to go to New Orleans, which I wish I had never done, I wound up with guys at QB like Danny Wuerffel, Billy Joe Tolliver, and Jake Delhomme his rookie year. In Tampa I had Shaun King, all good guys but not the talent at the quarterback position like I had in Pittsburgh."

Following the 1996 season Hastings left the Steelers via free agency for New Orleans. In his first season there he stayed productive despite playing for a team that went 6-10.

He had 48 catches for 722 yards and five scores. He remained with the Saints for two more years before wrapping up his career with Tampa Bay in 2000.

Hastings will always remember his time with the Steelers with fond memories, even wishing it wouldn't have ended as it did leaving after 1996.

"I wish I would have been able to stay and play my whole career there," Hastings said.

When it came to being a household name, even though he wasn't able to finish the job in Super Bowl XXX, fans in Pittsburgh remember Hastings and his contributions during his tenure with the team.

"Being in Pittsburgh there's no way not to be known, and I am not talking about not just the starters, but everyone on the team," Hastings said. "The support was always there from the fans, there's just such a historic tradition with the Steelers."

# CHAPTER 21

# BARRY FOSTER

### Running Back 1990–1994
#### September 13, 1992 vs New York Jets at Three Rivers Stadium
#### PITTSBURGH STEELERS 27 - NEW YORK JETS 10

When you think of great running backs for the Pittsburgh Steelers, the names roll off the tongue rather easily.

Franco Harris, John Henry Johnson, Willie Parker, Jerome Bettis, to even now with superstar back Le'Veon Bell.

One player, though, had one season in which he was better than all those names mentioned above, and that was the 1992 season turned in by back Barry Foster.

Amply nicknamed Barry "Bananas" Foster by ESPN mainstay Chris Berman, it wasn't unusual to see Foster in a number of highlights during that 1992 season, the first for head coach Bill Cowher.

Foster put up 1,690 yards rushing in 1992, doing it on 390 carries, at 4.3 yards per carry. He scored eleven touchdowns as the Steelers marched to an 11-5 record, good enough for the number one seed in the AFC.

The Steelers drafted Foster in the fifth round of the 1990 draft out of the College of Arkansas, where he put up 6.1 yards per carry in his senior season, rushing for 936 yards with nine touchdowns.

Once he got to the Steelers, he played mostly special teams in his rookie season, and by 1991 was able to get some carries, but it wasn't easy to break into the lineup.

"My first couple of seasons I was the backup to Merril Hoge, so I was kind of glad that Bill Cowher, who came in in 1992, brought in an offensive coordinator in Ron Erhardt who was committed to running the football," Foster said.

With Hoge as the starter in 1991, Foster did play in ten games, starting nine, and rushed for 488 yards and a score, including a 121-yard game early in the season against Buffalo.

"There were some talented guys in front of me. Merril [Hoge] was a very talented player, productive player," Foster said.

"We had Tim Worley, big-time running back, and he was doing some good things on the field, some bad things off the field, but was still super talented.

It was hard for me coming in to take those guys' positions, and really get consistent playing time. At that time we were in a different offense, it was a two tight end oriented offense."

At the time the Steelers had an offensive coordinator in Joe Walton, a former head coach of the New York Jets who was set in his ways, and didn't seem to waver no matter how bad things were going.

To document how bad Walton's offense struggled, the team didn't score an offensive touchdown until the fifth week of the 1990 season.

The team did get the ship right, but still missed the playoffs, going 9-7 and falling in a winner-take-all game in Week 16 with the Houston Oilers in Houston, losing 34-14.

It wasn't a stretch to figure out that Foster wasn't a fan of the offense Walton ran, as the terminology was a head scratcher for a lot of the players.

"Joe Walton was our offensive coordinator, and to be honest that offense was very confusing," Foster said.

"Not only for me as a rookie and second-year player, but for all the veteran players too.

"I remember being in a team meeting, and every position, we were all confused. At that time I hadn't really gotten a good handle on the offense and to be honest I was making a lot of mistakes.

"Another thing that really prevented me from playing as much as I should have was that Joe was a big fan of Merril Hoge. He absolutely loved Merril Hoge and they are still good friends to this day.

AP Photo/George Widman

# Notes on Barry Foster

| | |
|---|---|
| **Years Played:** | 1990–1994 |
| **Position:** | Running Back |
| **Height:** | 5'10" |
| **Weight:** | 223 |
| **Hometown:** | Hurst, Texas |
| **Current Residence:** | Dallas, Texas |
| **Occupation:** | Middle School Gym Teacher |
| **Accomplishments:** | Played college ball at Arkansas, where in three seasons he rushed for 2,080 yards and 20 touchdowns, including nine his final season before going into the NFL Draft. Was selected by the Steelers in the fifth round, 128th pick overall, in the 1990 NFL Draft. Played mostly special teams his rookie season and two years later was named the feature back in Bill Cowher's first season as coach. Ran for a single-season Steelers record 1690 yards in 1992, tying Eric Dickerson's record with twelve 100-yard rushing games. Finished 1992 as the AFC top rusher and second to Emmitt Smith by 23 yards for the rushing title, and was voted to the Pro Bowl with 11 touchdowns. In 1993 ran for 711 yards and nine touchdowns, but was limited to nine games with an ankle injury. Was part of the NFL's number one rushing attack in 1994, and ran for 851 total yards, including a 179-yard effort early in the year at home against the Colts. Was traded to the Carolina Panthers before the 1995 season, but never played a down for the Panthers after failing his physical. Retired from the game at age twenty-six with 3,943 yards and 28 total touchdowns. |
| **Nickname:** | "Bananas" |
| **The Game:** | Pittsburgh Steelers vs New York Jets in Pittsburgh, Pennsylvania<br>September 13, 1992 |

"That was his guy, and it was really hard for me to win Joe over as offensive coordinator and take away any playing time from Merril Hoge. The playing time that I did get, I have to credit Chuck Noll.

"Chuck would have to consistently get on Joe Walton's behind about putting me in games, even though when he put me in at certain times I produced, and at certain times I didn't."

When Cowher came in for the 1992 season as the new coach, he brought with him Ron Erhardt, an old coordinator of the New York Giants who loved to do one thing—run the football.

That opportunity gave Foster his chance, and he was named the starter in the 1992 season. He broke out of the gates with a 107-yard effort and a score as the Steelers upset the Oilers 29-24 at the Astrodome.

"It's really hard to foresee a season like that. Obviously for me it was just exciting for me to be considered a starter," Foster said.

"They had made that commitment and were looking for me to be that workhorse. I was just excited to be able to showcase my running abilities.

"It was really hard to be as successful as I was going to be that season, I was just happy to be a starter to be honest."

The best was to come for Foster in 1992, starting with the Steelers home opener in a Week 2 home game against the New York Jets.

# The Game

*By Barry Foster*

That 1992 season, that was the best season I had as a professional running back, and there were quite a few games that were memorable.

For me, that special game was our Week 2 game at home against the New York Jets.

In this particular game I ended up with 190 yards, which is the most yards I ever rushed for in an NFL game. But what really made it special for me was that I had three fumbles in that game.

That was the point where Bill Cowher came to me during the game. After that third fumble I was sitting there on the sidelines, and as a running back three fumbles in a game, that's pretty bad.

Yet, I was still rushing and scoring touchdowns, and Bill Cowher came up to me and he was talking to me on the sidelines and he was like, "Hey, don't worry about the fumbles, you are our running back. We can't win without you; we need you for this thing to work."

It was just that kind of validation for me to sit there and say, "Okay this organization is counting on me, my teammates are counting on me, the coaching staff is counting on me." It was just really a point where I felt accepted, and I was really a part of their plans and what they were trying to do to lead the Pittsburgh Steelers to successful season after successful season.

That particular game against the Jets is one that really just kind of stands out because it validated my importance to the Pittsburgh Steelers organization and the coaching staff at the time.

We had a great offensive line, they were good pass blockers, but their specialty was to get out and run block. Those guys on the line were just amazing at that.

I can't imagine another center who could snap the ball, and pull, and be the lead blocker on the outside as good as Dermontti Dawson. The guy was amazing; that's why he's in the Hall of Fame.

You also have to mention Duval Love, he was one of those linemen that could get out there and run block.

It couldn't have worked out any better for me, and for running backs like Bam Morris and Jerome Bettis. Those guys were blessed with just God given ability to get out and run.

From having Ron Erhardt run his New York Giants run-oriented offense to that offensive line to having myself, Merril Hoge, and the other running backs to just plug into place, I think it was just perfect timing for the Steelers to have success running the ball with the offensive lineman and the running backs that we had.

Back to that game, I remember the 54-yard touchdown run that put us ahead for good early in the fourth quarter.

Obviously anytime you can make a big play that's going to help solidify the win, or help win the game. It's huge. It was just a good play for our team at the time.

It just made me feel a little bit better because I had already made so many mistakes earlier in the game with those fumbles, so for me it was sweeter just to kind of wash out that bad taste I had in my mouth.

Having that run was a personal victory for me, and for the team to go on for the victory.

I've been asked about being in the "zone" that day, and I didn't really think that's a game that I can say I was in the "zone," but I had a good feeling.

My offensive lineman were really blocking their tails off, and it helped that I was getting chunks of yards on my runs also.

Actually, I felt like I was out of the "zone" for that particular game because I normally would never have three fumbles in one game.

I remember sitting on the sidelines after fumbles one and two and then three, and trying to really get a grasp of what I was doing and what was going on, thinking, "I've got three fumbles here, what's the problem?" I remember just sitting there wondering what I was doing to cause those fumbles, and it really helped when Bill came over and talked to me about them.

In that particular game it ended up well statistically for me, but I wouldn't consider that game as a game that I felt I was in the zone even though I had 190 yards rushing.

## The Aftermath

The 1992 Steelers were a young group led by a young coach who took a team that had gone 7-9 the season before and pushed them to heights that many felt were not possible.

The club was led by an amazing season for Foster, who not only broke the single-season record for 1,692 yards, but also tied Eric Dickerson's record for most 100-yard games in a season with 12.

The defining game of the season for the Steelers came in Week 9, when they had a critical home affair with the Oilers.

Both teams came in at 5-2, and many felt the winner would have clear control of the division with seven weeks left in the season.

Down 20-7 in the third quarter, the Steelers rallied for two fourth-quarter touchdowns, and an Al Del Greco missed field goal in the final seconds sealed a 21-20 Steelers victory.

Foster rushed for 118 yards that afternoon, again leading the ground game which had been the biggest staple to the team's offense in 1992.

While the Steelers were winning, Cowher was solidifying his place in the hearts of Steelers fans worldwide.

His ability to pull players aside during the game and calm them down was an asset that hadn't been seen under Chuck Noll, who was usually very stoic on the sidelines.

Foster wasn't the only player Cowher had come to during the game. More than once cameras caught him talking to players like Rod Woodson, Greg Lloyd, and a number of others, telling them to stay focused.

"Being a player's coach, that's one of the many strengths Bill Cowher has. He can relate to his players on how to play professional football," Foster said.

"He was a linebacker for the Browns, and he has that ability to come to a player, and calm that player down.

"That's one of the first things that impressed me the first time I met and hung out on the field with Bill Cowher, the fact he was all about his team, and he's a great players' coach.

"That's what players look for in a coach, someone who can relate to them, to keep them motivated to get better, and produce at the end as far as wins."

The 1992 season ended for the Steelers in the divisional round in a tough home loss to the Buffalo Bills.

The 24-3 score does not indicate the closeness of the game, as Buffalo scored 10 points in the final quarter to cement the win.

Foster was a rising star in the NFL, a player entering his prime coming off a record season. In 1993 he was having another solid season, but an ankle injury suffered in a Week 9 win over the Bills ended his season.

The 1994 season Foster split time with rookie Byron "Bam" Morris, as the team led the league in rushing.

The pair combined for 1,687 yards and 12 touchdowns as the 12-4 Steelers wound up as the number one seed in the AFC, then dominated Cleveland in the AFC Divisional Game at Three Rivers Stadium 29-9.

Heavy favorites the following week at home against the San Diego Chargers, the wet turf from a rare balmy January day combined with a stingy Chargers defense held the Steelers to just 66 yards rushing in a crushing 17-13 defeat.

The final offensive play for the Steelers came at the Chargers' 3-yard line. Quarterback Neil O'Donnell, who set numerous AFC Title Game records in the loss, dropped back and tried to quickly hit Foster with a pass in the end zone.

The back started to slide to the turf, and Chargers linebacker Dennis Gibson came over the top, knocking the ball away and ending the Steelers' hopes of a trip to the Super Bowl.

Little did anyone know it would be the last play Foster would ever play for the Steelers, or in the NFL in a game other than the preseason.

That offseason the running back, who was just twenty-six years old, was traded for a sixth-round pick to the newly created Carolina Panthers.

He appeared in some preseason action for Carolina, but the franchise released him after he failed a physical.

Instead of trying to find another club, the back decided he had done enough, and walked away from the game.

He did have a brief comeback with the Cincinnati Bengals that lasted just days, but after a workout in pads he decided he just didn't have the desire to play anymore.

Foster's career may have only spanned five seasons, but many fans will never forget his magical season of 1992, a season where he was right at the top of being the best running back in the NFL.

# CHAPTER 22

# NORM JOHNSON

### Kicker 1995–1998
#### January 28, 1996 vs Dallas Cowboys at Sun Devil Stadium
#### DALLAS COWBOYS 27 - PITTSBURGH STEELERS 17

When the Pittsburgh Steelers were getting set for their 1995 season, veteran kicker Norm Johnson was not on the team's roster. He wasn't even on the team's radar.

The Steelers, coming off a 12-4 season in 1994 and a heartbreaking loss in the AFC Title Game to the San Diego Chargers, had signed veteran kicker Dean Biasucci at the end of June. He was going to take over the kicker position for the departed Gary Anderson.

The problem was Biasucci, who was coming off ten seasons with the Indianapolis Colts, was awful in the preseason, and after he missed four field goals in an August preseason game at Tampa Bay, the Steelers waived him.

Enter Norm Johnson.

Johnson was already a thirteen-year veteran when the Steelers inked him after releasing Biasucci, and right away he was exposed to new experiences in Pittsburgh.

"When I came to the Steelers from Atlanta, and signed with the Steelers, my first day when I flew in and was walking through the airport in Pittsburgh I was recognized," Johnson remembers. "No uniform, no helmet. I was just blown away by that."

He played four seasons in the Steel City, and it was a rabid fan base that sparked some of the most vivid memories for Johnson, along with a popular television show.

"I have actually for the most part pretty fond memories of my time in Pittsburgh," Johnson said. "I was well received by the fan base; it's such a tremendous fan base.

"That was the first team that I had really played with that had a fan base that when we traveled they would show up at the airport wherever we played. That was a new experience for me, and was actually quite cool."

The television show that had a connection with Johnson was the NBC hit *Cheers*, which was a popular show from 1982 to 1993, and then had a long run in syndication.

When Johnson made a field goal at Three Rivers Stadium, the Steelers showed a clip from the show on the scoreboard that hit home with the kicker.

"I was a big fan of the TV show *Cheers*, and I remember the Steelers had to go to NBC, who controlled the rights for *Cheers*, and they got permission to run the clip of the character Norm walking into the bar and everyone yelling 'Norm!' every time I made a field goal at home," Johnson recalls.

"That was actually pretty darn cool as I was a big fan of the show. That was also an experience that I had never had before."

It didn't take long for fans to take to Johnson, as his first year with the franchise he led the NFL in field goals made (34) and attempted (41), and put up a career-high 141 points.

He and the Steelers did get revenge on their 1994 AFC Title Game loss, reaching the postseason with an 11-5 record, beating the Buffalo Bills 40-21 in the AFC Divisional Playoff Game, and then outlasting the Indianapolis Colts 20-16 in the AFC Title Game.

The win earned them a trip to Tempe, Arizona, for a Super Bowl XXX matchup with the Dallas Cowboys, who came in as heavy favorites to top the Steelers.

It was a moment in time for Johnson that he still recalls fondly, along with a surprise play that almost turned the tide for good for the Steelers.

AP Photo/Gene J. Puskar

# Notes on Norm Johnson

| | |
|---|---|
| **Years Played:** | 1995–1998 |
| **Position:** | Kicker |
| **Height:** | 6'2" |
| **Weight:** | 202 |
| **Hometown:** | Inglewood, California |
| **Current Residence:** | Seattle, Washington |
| **Occupation:** | Real estate agent and owner of Peak Personality Performance |
| **Accomplishments:** | Played his college ball at UCLA before kicking for the Seattle Seahawks for nine seasons and the Atlanta Falcons for four before joining the Steelers prior to the 1995 campaign. Graduated in 1983 with a bachelor's degree in economics from UCLA. Played for a total of eighteen NFL seasons with Seattle, Atlanta, Pittsburgh, and Philadelphia. Hit on 366 of 477 field goals over eighteen seasons, a percentage of 76.7, and made 638 of 644 extra points throughout his career. Led the NFL in both field goals made (34) and attempted (41), and hit on all 39 extra point attempts in his first season in Pittsburgh in 1995, leading the AFC in scoring. Was the first kicker to successfully execute a "surprise onside" kick in a Super Bowl in Super Bowl XXX vs Dallas in January of 1996. Attempted two punts in his career, one each in 1991 and 1992 as a member of the Falcons. |
| **Nickname:** | None |
| **The Game:** | Pittsburgh Steelers vs Dallas Cowboys in Tempe, Arizona<br>January 28, 1996 |

# The Game
*By Norm Johnson*

We were big underdogs going into that Super Bowl.

You look back and you're playing one of the greatest quarterbacks of all time in Troy Aikman, they say one of the best offensive lines of all time, and Emmitt Smith the leading NFL rusher of all time.

When we won the AFC Championship Game against the Indianapolis Colts, which was a very tight game, it was a last second game that could have gone either way.

It was really an emotional roller coaster that could have gone either way, but we won that game.

We had two weeks between that game and the Super Bowl, and I remember that first week having huge anxiety.

What started to go through my head was how huge a stage that game was, and how millions and millions of people were going to see this.

I started thinking, "I've played for fourteen seasons, but millions and millions of people are going to watch this, and will judge me and my fourteen years on just one game, and maybe even one play."

It's so easy to judge a kicker. You don't know about the snapper or the holder, the ground where you kick, but you know if he made it or missed it.

So I was thinking, "Holy cow, I've got millions and millions and millions of people that are going to judge me on possibly one play." I started to carry that weight around and I really had a lot of anxiety.

I talked to some people and started to feel better, and then the second week we had all the media and what not, and then it was lockdown, practice, concentrate on football; the second week was easy.

Going into the game it was easy, once you step on the field you kind of block out everything else and you're just playing football.

Before that field goal, there was anxiety. It was a long field goal, but we did need it, and it was on grass. Most grass stadiums at the end of the year are not in great shape.

They make the fields look good at the end of the season for TV, but when you're down on the field playing there's a lot of loose turf.

Sometimes they even paint dirt green. I've been on fields where they fill holes with green sand.

That may work when you're running or blocking or tackling, but it's not very good for a kicker.

So we were losing the game 20-7 in the fourth quarter, and I went out and hit a 46-yard field goal, a kick which went off without a hitch, worked perfectly.

Then I had about a minute and twenty seconds to prepare for the biggest surprise trick play of my career.

It was a surprise onside kick: the first successful surprise onside kick in a Super Bowl, first even attempted surprise onside kick in a Super Bowl.

I was pretty proud of that, it's not an easy thing to do. It worked out well on the biggest stage in football.

Right before it I hit the 46-yard field goal, which along with it came a little bit of anxiety, coming on that big stage.

That game and that onside kick the NFL Network used in their "Top 10 Gutsiest Calls." It came in at number eight but they told me that it would have been much higher if we would have won.

That play really gave us a chance. It turned the momentum of the game around, turned the crowd around.

That kick was not something used very often, but it was something that I practiced earlier in my career, back when I played with the Seahawks.

I'm not sure we ever used it, but we worked on it.

Bobby April, was the special teams coach with the Steelers, his first year in the league he was with the Atlanta Falcons. I was there his first year in the league in Atlanta.

We got along great. He's a great guy and he makes playing the game fun. I showed him how I had practiced that particular onside kick.

He liked it. He knew that I had the ability to do that.

Leading up to the game, it was not something I had practiced a lot, but it was a lot like riding a bicycle. So leading up to the Super Bowl the coaches said, "Hey we see this opportunity here." I was thinking, "Oh right, as if we are going to use this in the Super Bowl." I practiced it a little bit, but I don't even remember if we practiced it much the week of the Super Bowl. We must have done it a couple times in practice.

I still thought there was no chance we would call something like that in the Super Bowl.

I went in to kick the field goal, and that was where a conversation took place with Bill Cowher and the coaches. I had no idea about that, I was not part of that decision to try the onside.

After that field goal I came off the sideline and I joined the huddle for the kickoff team, and all of a sudden I heard "surprise onside right." My mouth just dropped right there on the sideline. I said to myself, "Are you kidding me?!" There were a couple of things that go into that kick. You have to make it look like you are kicking deep. So you can't do anything really drastic to make it look like something is up.

I remember approaching the ball, and I was trying to concentrate. All of a sudden I saw out of my peripheral vision a player from the Cowboys running back.

Well, I would rather have not have seen that. It threw my attention as I was approaching the ball, and as I was trying to do this.

Luckily everything just kind of went into auto-mode and it went off without a hitch. Looking back on it I think, "Holy cow, I lost my focus because I saw this guy move." I remember thinking about it and I can still see him running away and of course you're not supposed to notice anything. It's like lining up for a field goal and you notice something that you're supposed to block out.

It's like in basketball when you are trying a free throw and you notice something when you are supposed to be in the zone.

I could have totally blown the kick, but in the end it worked out perfectly.

Deon Figures, one of our cornerbacks recovered the kick for us, the ball popped up perfectly in his stomach. He actually kept running down the field but you can't advance it. It made the crowd go wild.

That's one of the highlight plays, and certainly highlight games of my career. I just wish we would have been able to capitalize on it enough to turn the game around for good.

## The Aftermath

Steelers fans to this day recall the disappointment of the loss of Super Bowl XXX, and along with it the two key interceptions from quarterback Neil O'Donnell that directly led to 14 Cowboys points.

The onside kick led to a Steelers touchdown from running back Bam Morris that put the Steelers within three at 20-17 with plenty of time left in the fourth quarter.

The Steelers got the ball back with a shot to possibly win the game with 4:15 left at their own 32-yard line.

After an incomplete pass, O'Donnell's next pass was thrown right to Cowboys cornerback Larry Brown, who took the pick back to the Steelers 6-yard line.

Two plays later, Emmitt Smith went over for the clinching score, leaving Steelers fans stunned as to why O'Donnell's pass was thrown totally to the wrong spot on the field. Wide receiver Andre Hastings appeared to be running a slant, and O'Donnell threw it to the outside.

While the play continues to be questioned by Steelers fans, Johnson himself doesn't know why there was such miscommunication on the play and who was at fault.

"The crazy thing from my standpoint as a kicker, I'm not in the offensive meetings to begin with. I'm not in receiver meetings, I'm not in quarterback meetings, I'm in special teams meetings," Johnson said.

"So after the Super Bowl, there's no more meetings. At the end of the season you go home, you're around for a day or two and then you're off.

"It's not like you're back at work for another week, you're done. So I never got an explanation of what happened—and I was a teammate.

"I was on the team and stayed on the team for an additional three years. I still to this day don't know what happened and why that took place."

It was a bitter pill to swallow, and for Johnson it was his only appearance in a Super Bowl in his eighteen NFL seasons.

He kicked with the Steelers for three more seasons, and still holds the single season scoring record for the Steelers with 141 points in 1995, and most field goals in a season with 34 in 1995.

Johnson ended his career with a season in Philadelphia in 1999, wrapping up a solid eighteen years in the NFL in which he kicked a total of 1,736 points.

He still recalls the 1995 season, his first and best in Pittsburgh, with warm memories.

"Despite the loss in that Super Bowl, I wear my 1995 championship ring to this day," Johnson said.

# CHAPTER 23

# CRAIG COLQUITT

### Punter 1978–1984

#### August 5, 1978 vs Baltimore Colts at Memorial Stadium
#### PITTSBURGH STEELERS 22 - BALTIMORE COLTS 10

The job of being a punter in the NFL is a very unforgiving one. Much like that of an offensive lineman, about the only time your name gets mentioned is when you do something bad.

For former Steelers punter Craig Colquitt, he's lived most of his life having to hear about punting, both good and bad.

He's not only a two-time Super Bowl champion punter for the Pittsburgh Steelers, but he's also the father of two punters currently in the NFL, Dustin (Kansas City Chiefs), and Britton (Denver Broncos).

The ride to the NFL for Colquitt was an interesting one. He kicked at the University of Tennessee, and then sat back in the 1978 NFL Draft to see if he was going to be one of the lucky ones selected.

He felt like he would go somewhere, but had no idea just how high he would end up, going in the third round to the Steelers.

"I had no ego or knowledge of it whatsoever," Colquitt said. "Back then you didn't have any internet, your research was the library or what people passed down to you.

*Courtesy of the Pittsburgh Steelers*

# Notes on Craig Colquitt

| | |
|---|---|
| **Years Played:** | 1978–1984 |
| **Position:** | Punter |
| **Height:** | 6'1" |
| **Weight:** | 182 |
| **Hometown:** | Knoxville, Tennessee |
| **Current Residence:** | Lebanon, Tennessee |
| **Occupation:** | Senior Representative at GCA Services |
| **Accomplishments:** | Went to college at Tennessee, and was the Steelers third-round pick of the 1978 NFL Draft. Played seven seasons in the NFL, the first six with the Steelers (1978–84), then returned to the game for a brief stint with the Indianapolis Colts (1987). Averaged 41.3 yards per punt in those seasons. He did not have a punt blocked until his brief tenure with the Colts. Was one of the first punters to take two steps instead of three before punting. Played in ninety-seven games over his NFL career. Best season was 1983 when he punted 80 times and averaged 41.9 yards per kick. Had a career-long 74-yard punt in 1981. Was inducted into the Greater Knoxville Hall of Fame in July of 2009. Two sons, Britton (Denver Broncos) and Dustin (Kansas City Chiefs), both are current NFL punters. |
| **Nickname:** | None |
| **The Game:** | Pittsburgh Steelers vs Baltimore Colts in Baltimore, Maryland August 5, 1978 |

"I was told the day before by the Dallas Cowboys that they were going to draft me in the fifth round. I was thrilled, I wanted to be a Dallas Cowboy.

"Honestly I was disappointed when I was drafted by the Steelers, until Joe Gordon called me, their PR Director, and he asked me questions like, 'What's it feel like to play with players like Terry Bradshaw, Lynn Swann, Franco Harris, Jack Lambert, Mike Webster?' He went through all these names and I got emotional.

"I hadn't thought of it that way, and as it worked out, Dallas never beat us when it went on the record. They beat us in exhibition, but they never beat us when it counted. We played them that year in the 1978 season in the Super Bowl in Miami and we won."

It did not start all that easy for the third-round pick, as his first training camp included stiff competition for the Steelers punting position.

The first preseason game for Colquitt was a test of nerves and endurance, as he had to not only try to impress with his leg, but get past the mental part of trying to make the team that was a dynasty in the making.

# The Game

*By Craig Colquitt*

My most memorable game would have to be first game I ever played in, the first game of the preseason to start the 1978 season.

We played in Baltimore, and I had five competitors going up against me for the punting position. Everybody got a chance to kick in the game.

I was most concerned about a guy who was not only a punter but also a tight end. I was a third-round draft choice, but I was more concerned about him than all the other guys.

As it panned out, I did terribly in that game, but not as terribly as everybody else. Stage fright is an interesting creature; it reduces a whole lot of your body parts and makes them all tight.

I was under significant pressure. I just felt it from being picked in the third round, and also because I had competition, I had never had competition before until I got to the NFL.

Before that game I was looking around at guys and I noticed they were out of character. They were very tense, and they actually ignored me.

We were kind of chummy and not chummy because of the situation in training camp. When it came to show time, I think everybody kind of realized it was make it or break it.

They didn't want distractions.

I can only remember me punting one time in the game, and I remember Chuck Noll really liked punting side to side to minimize returns.

My punt that game, it didn't spiral, it helicoptered, it went end over end, it did everything as a punter you didn't want it to do, but it did go 42 or 45 yards and went out of bounds.

I was kicking to the left, which Chuck wanted me to do, and there was no return so I accomplished my task.

I do recall the guy I was most concerned about, the tight end, he took the snap from center and tried to get control of the ball and couldn't, and was waylaid by three or four opponents.

He never got his kick off, and came right to the sidelines and came right to me, after he had ignored me the whole pregame and what not. It would have been a lot easier if everyone had just been having a good time.

He came up to me and said, "I guess you got the job." I felt like I had the job at that point. After watching their performances, as bad as mine was, theirs was horrible.

Those guys were gone as soon as we got to training camp on Sunday. We played on Saturday and came back on Sunday and I was alone after that.

At that point it was just me and kicker Roy Gerela, and I could just focus on what I had to do.

It was a completely different atmosphere because the rosters were starting to get cut, and people were really starting to support each other.

## The Aftermath

The 1978 Steelers squad was one of the best teams in the history of the franchise. The club lost just two games, falling in Week 8 at home to the Houston Oilers, and three weeks later they lost a 10-7 Sunday night game to the Los Angeles Rams.

Other than those two blemishes, the Steelers were dominant. They went 14-2 in the regular season, and then outscored the Denver Broncos and Houston Oilers 67-15 in two playoff games to reach Super Bowl XIII.

The thirteenth Super Bowl was a rematch with the team that called itself "America's Team," the Dallas Cowboys.

It was one of the greatest games in the history of the NFL, and it was a game that Colquitt can still recall with great detail.

"As we were arriving at the stadium, the bus was completely surrounded by black and gold fans. They were wearing black and gold and painted all up black and gold, and they were even pushing the bus, making it rock," Colquitt said.

"That wasn't good for me as I was already anxious, and I didn't need it to get any worse. I'm a Christian, and I have these beliefs and theories and stuff in pregame warm-ups, and I knew that God was going to come down out of the clouds.

"I had a good game. I had a punt that went 52 yards in that game, and it got returned a little bit. I saw the effort that day being made by my teammates defensively and offensively and it just kicked me into another gear."

The effort the team put forth was worthy of the championship, as they built a 35-17 fourth quarter lead.

Despite a spirited comeback from Hall of Fame Dallas quarterback Roger Staubach, the Steelers outlasted the Cowboys 35-31.

Colquitt's first season in the NFL saw him punt 66 times and average exactly 40 yards per punt.

The next season the team again reached the summit, winning their second straight title and fourth in six seasons.

A 31-19 win in Super Bowl XIV over the Los Angeles Rams capped off the amazing run by the Steelers dynasty, but it wasn't the end for Colquitt, who lasted with the team until following the 1984 season.

He had a productive six seasons with the Steelers, averaging 41.3 yards per punt, with a career-best of 43.3 yards per punt in the 1981 campaign.

"It's humbling and fulfilling in the same token, but then you have to do it in the next week and then the next week and the next week," Colquitt said.

He remembers with great fondness the great players and coaches in Pittsburgh he had the honor of playing with, and winning two championships with his first two seasons in the league in 1978 and 1979.

"They were amazing, just amazing people. I tell people all the time we were all young. The guys they were incredibly professional, they gave it their best; it was fun to be around. It was the best opportunity in my lifetime," Colquitt said.

That's not the end of the story for the former Steelers punter by a longshot. He has two sons, both of whom are punters, and both of whom are on rosters in the NFL.

Dustin Colquitt has been the punter for the Kansas City Chiefs since 2005, while Britton Colquitt plays in the same AFC West division as his brother with the Denver Broncos.

There's even a cousin in the mix, Jimmy Colquitt, who is the career leader in punting at the University of Tennessee, where all the Colquitts played in college.

It's not often in the NFL that you can have a legacy of multiple children playing in the NFL, but for Colquitt, he's had the privilege of taking what was his dream and now watching it through his children.

# ACKNOWLEDGMENTS

First and foremost I dedicate this book to my Lord and Savior, Jesus Christ, for without him, none of this would be possible. To my loving wife, Shanna, who has always been a great source of encouragement and has always stood by me through the ups and downs of this project.

To my loving family, my mom and dad for their loving support, brothers John, Russell, and Michael, sisters-in-law Mary Ann, Terri, and Kim, and eight nieces and nephews for their love through the years. To my wonderful in-laws for their support and understanding about not being around as much as I would like pursuing my dreams in this crazy career.

To Steeler Nation—the best fans in the NFL. To my friends for their help in this project, Darren McFarland, Christina Rivers, and Vince Miller, and friends Charles Spooner, Steven Spooner, Melanie Cramer, Josh Thompson, Dave Hummel, Lindsey Foltin, T.J. Zuppe, Tim Alcorn, Greg Buk, Ed Emrich, Steve Emrich, Karl Jeske, Ryan Kaczmarski, Jim Koney, Paul Loede, Dan McVey, Joe Simonetta, Kate Mueller, Sujeet Patel, John Sefcik, Matt Sefcik, and the best karate teacher ever in Mark Miller, as well as everyone else who was kind enough to take the time in helping me get in touch with players who contributed to this book.

And finally to my church family at Cleveland Baptist Church for always keeping my feet on the ground. Pastor Kevin Folger, Pete Folger, Jack Beaver, Ron Van Kirk, Doug Schweitzer, Jeremy Cron, Tim Kardamis, Tim Hanrahan, Ryan Zapsic, Bill Yeager, Al Varwig, and all the rest. Thank you for all your support.